St Mary's Clapham

The Church of Our Immaculate Lady of Victories
and its Redemptorist Community

Text by
Brendan McConvery C.Ss.R.

Photography by
Jess Esposito

Design by
Tanika Design

Published by Redemptorist Publications
Alphonsus House, Chawton, Hampshire, GU34 3HQ, UK
Tel. +44 (0)1420 88222, Fax. +44 (0)1420 88805
Email rp@rpbooks.co.uk, www.rpbooks.co.uk

A registered charity limited by guarantee
Registered in England 3261721
Copyright © Redemptorist Publications 2016

Edited by Therese Garman SMP

ISBN 978-0-85231-470-8

All rights reserved. No part of this publication may be reproduced, stored in a retrieval system, or transmitted in any form or by any means, electronic, mechanical, photocopying, recording or otherwise, without prior permission in writing from Redemptorist Publications.

The moral right of Brendan McConvery CSsR to be identified as the author of this work has been asserted in accordance with the Copyright, Designs and Patents Act 1988.

Every effort has been made to trace copyright holders and to obtain their permission for the use of copyright material. The publisher apologises for any errors or omissions and would be grateful for notification of any corrections that should be incorporated in future reprints or editions of this book.

A CIP catalogue record for this book is available from the British Library.

The publisher gratefully acknowledges permission to use the following copyright material:

Excerpts from the English translation and chants of *The Roman Missal* © 2010, International Commission on English in the Liturgy Corporation. All rights reserved.

Excerpts from the *New Revised Standard Version of the Bible: Anglicised Edition*, © 1989, 1995, Division of Christian Education of the National Council of the Churches of Christ in the United States of America. Used by permission. All rights reserved.

Printed by Portland Print, Kettering, NN16 8UN

Contents

Introduction by Fr Richard Reid C.Ss.R	1
Letter from Archbishop Peter Smith	2
Letter from Fr Michael Brehl C.Ss.R	3
Chapter 1: A Catholic Church for Clapham	5
Chapter 2: Growing Parish, Expanding Church	15
Chapter 3: The Redemptorists	31
Chapter 4: Architects and Artists	45
Chapter 5: Guide to the Church	51
Appendix: Work on the Church Spire 2015	83
Acknowledgements	86

Redemptorist Publications would like to acknowledge the generous support of the Heritage Lottery Fund and the National Churches Trust

Introduction by Fr Richard Reid, Rector of St Mary's

The Redemptorists have been in Clapham since 1848. Often I stand at the bottom of the garden and look up to the monastery and the church, with the spire towering over the neighbourhood, and I appreciate somewhat the story of this Redemptorist building and place. I allow my mind to go back many years, long even before I was born, and envisage the many Redemptorist Fathers and Brothers of yesteryear living their daily life here in Clapham. From the stories older *confrères* tell, from the writings in old chronicles recording both the humdrum events of daily life and the more memorable moments, it is easy to imagine a face at a window, to see someone pass in the corridor or someone in the garden, saying the rosary as they walk. Strange as this may sound, it is easy to do this as, in some ways, St Mary's has not changed much in the past hundred years.

Fr Richard Reid C.Ss.R

More to the point the Redemptorists are still going about their daily ministry, as were those of many years ago. It is also interesting to observe, that, as it was in its beginnings, our community is still made up of men of different nationalities and of a wide range of ages. At present, living, working and praying in this monastery, we are thirteen Redemptorists from England, India, Ireland, Scotland and Zimbabwe, ranging in age from twenty-seven to eighty-six years old.

We stand on the shoulders of those who have gone before us, and their story is told here with honesty, precision and great affection by Fr Brendan McConvery C.Ss.R. It is a story of adventure, of new beginnings, but always of faithfulness to the Lord and to the Redemptorist way of life. Turning the pages, one senses that these men are still alive and well and going about their priestly and religious work.

It should also be noted that something of the history of Clapham is to be found within these pages. As the story of the Redemptorists is told, so is the story of the people of Clapham, and as such, we are glad to have this book as a wider history of this wonderful area we live in.

This book would not have been written were it not for the major work carried out on our spire, which has been such a landmark in this area for the past 165 years. For all the people who helped us in so many ways, we are grateful. That gratitude extends to Fergus McCormick, senior architect in charge of the project and his colleagues, to the Heritage Lottery Fund, The National Churches Trust Fund and the good people of Clapham and our Redemptorist Friends who have given so generously.

Fr Richard Reid C.Ss.R
Rector St Mary's Clapham

Introduction

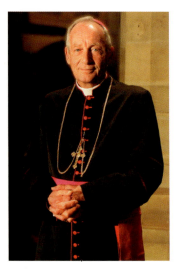

Archbishop Peter Smith

Letter from the Archbishop of Southwark

I was delighted to hear of the forthcoming publication of this new book on the history of St Mary's, Clapham and of the great work and the commitment that the resident Redemptorist communities and the parishioners have achieved over the past 167 years.

I must admit to a special fondness for St Mary's, because I went to the primary school for boys in St. Alphonsus Road in the early 1950s. The Parish Priest in those days was Fr Lucas, who frequently dropped into the school and circulated round the playground during our break times. He had a great charism in relating to us youngsters and was much admired for his wonderful sense of humour, his kindness and generosity. For me, Fr Lucas epitomised the fundamental charism of the Redemptorist Order and I shall always be eternally grateful for those early formative years which gave me such a good education and enabled me to be accepted for my secondary education at Clapham College.

So it is a delight to be able to read of the history of St Mary's, from its beginnings in the 1850s, when the Catholic Hierarchy was restored following the Reformation in the sixteenth century, and from which began what Blessed John Henry Newman described as "a new spring" in the life of the Catholic Church in this country. Fr Brendan McConvery C.Ss.R has written a fascinating and insightful history of the involvement of the Redemptorists, the bishops and archbishops of Southwark, the eminent architects and artists who played such an important role in the development of the church building, and the commitment of the parishioners, all of whom, in different ways, have contributed to the growth of the parish. It is a story of the vibrant faith of Catholics who, despite considerable difficulties and sometimes fierce opposition, built the church, the schools and a flourishing community of faith which continues to this day.

+ Peter Smith,
Archbishop of Southwark

Letter from Fr Michael Brehl

Fr Michael Brehl C.Ss.R
Superior General of the Redemptorist Congregation

St Mary's Clapham is probably after Sant'Alfonso and the Alphonsian Holy Places, one of the Redemptorist houses best known to Redemptorists worldwide. For many, it has been a place of welcome while they pursued studies in London, or learned English. For others, it has been a place of refuge from war or persecution in their home country. For others, it has been a place of rest for a day or two before beginning the next leg of their missionary journey. The founders of some of our most flourishing provinces in Africa and Asia enjoyed its hospitality before setting out to bring the Redemptorist witness to new places.

The Redemptorists came to Clapham at a time that Blessed John Henry Newman named "the Second Spring" for the Church in England. Some of the members of its earliest communities were associates of Newman or were at least touched by his Oxford Movement – men like Fr Edward Douglas who made the construction of the beautiful church possible by putting his inherited wealth at the disposal of the Congregation, something he was to do repeatedly in his lifetime, or Robert Coffin, convert Anglican priest, initially member of Newman's Oratory, then Redemptorist and finally, Bishop of Southwark, or Edward Bridgett, gifted writer and preacher. The Redemptorists were also enjoying their own 'second spring' at this time. The Congregation was attracting members at a higher rate than ever before in its history and was in an expansionist mood. It had already spread to Belgium, Holland, Germany and the United States. England proved to be another fertile mission field.

The Church of Our Lady of Victories is surely one of the most beautiful anywhere in the Congregation. Over the years love and care have been lavished upon it, not just by the Redemptorist priests and brothers who have served it for well over a century and a half. Several architects and artists have dedicated their skills to the glory of God. Nowhere can this be better seen than in the Lady Chapel. In this Jubilee Year of the Icon of Our Lady of Perpetual Help, it is particularly appropriate to remember how this corner of the church is truly a visual theology of the Mother of the Lord, our Mother of Perpetual Help. We must also remember the worshippers of Clapham down through the years. Rich and poor, old English and newly-arrived immigrants – Irish, Italian, Polish, West Indian, African and many others – have found it a place of welcome. Today St Mary's is still a flourishing parish with a regular round of activities both in the church and elsewhere.

I extend to the Redemptorists and people of St Mary's, Clapham my best wishes and prayers and I take this opportunity to thank them in the name of the world-wide Redemptorist family for their welcome to so many of us and their continued partnership with us in the mission of bringing the good news of "plentiful redemption" to the world.

In the Redeemer,
Michael Brehl, C.Ss.R.

1. A Catholic Church for Clapham

The Catholic Church in late eighteenth- and early nineteenth-century England was almost invisible. Neither England nor Scotland possessed a full Catholic episcopate.

They were ruled by a number of vicars apostolic, ordained as bishops but with few of the rights and privileges of diocesan bishops, and whose territory was extensive. Although the Catholic population of England had swollen from an estimated 80,000 in 1767 to almost ten times that by 1851, the vicars apostolic kept a low profile. Thomas Griffith, vicar apostolic of the London area from 1836 to 1847 was probably typical in his unwillingness to disturb the existing order of things. Although religious communities were beginning to arrive in England from the European mainland, he allowed none of them to open a public church. His immediate successor, Thomas Walsh, died after just a year in office and was succeeded by the energetic Nicholas Wiseman. Within a year of Wiseman's appointment, the hierarchy was restored and he was raised to the dignity of Cardinal Archbishop of Westminster, which dignity he retained until his death in 1865.

A new injection of life into the English Catholic Church came from a number of sources. Many Catholics fleeing the religious persecution of the *Reign of Terror* that followed the French Revolution in 1789 sought and found refuge in England. They were followed in the first part of the nineteenth century by refugees from revolutions elsewhere in Europe. That trickle became a tidal wave with the influx of refugees from the Irish Famine from 1845 onwards. On Wiseman's accession, there were just forty-two churches served by eighty-four priests in greater London: twenty years later, there were ninety-seven churches and 246 priests (an increase of more than 225 per cent and almost 300 per cent respectively). Wiseman positively encouraged male and female religious to come to his diocese, so that by 1889, there were fifty-three convents of women and twenty-four houses of religious men.

Clapham in the Nineteenth Century was a semi-rural place

There was another factor that could scarcely have been predicted. A group of learned Anglican clergymen, for the most part based in the University of Oxford, had begun to publish a series of ninety articles between 1833 and 1841, entitled *Tracts for the Times*. The purpose of the tracts was to restate the Catholic claims of the Anglican Church and to renew a deeper sacramental sense in the life and practice of Anglicanism. Its unforeseen result was a flow of Anglicans, lay and cleric, who, despairing of a thorough-going Catholic reform in their own church, sought to return to Rome.

Factors such as these were among the signs that the Roman Catholic Church in England in the 1850s was undergoing what Blessed John Henry Newman, who has become identified with the Oxford Movement, would call "the second spring".

Clapham

In the late eighteenth century, Clapham was a quiet semi-rural village on the edge of the city. Lavender Hill, not so very far away, acquired its name from the cultivation of fresh lavender as an ingredient for perfume. Around the Common, the homes of the comfortable middle classes were beginning to spring up. One particular group of Clapham residents were distinguished by their piety and the high moral line they took on issues such as slavery, then an economically significant element in British world trade. The "Clapham Saints", or "Clapham Sect", as they were popularly known, were a group of Evangelical Christians who worshipped in Holy Trinity Church on the Common. Their founder, Thomas Venn (after whom Venn Street, near St Mary's, is named) was a curate there and his son, John, later became its rector. The group included Zachary McAuley, father of (Lord) Thomas Babbington McAuley, the writer and historian, Lord Teignmouth, former governor general of India and first president of the British and Foreign Bible Society, and William Wilberforce, leader of the campaign for the abolition of slavery.

It has been estimated that at this time there were no more than thirty or forty Catholics in the Clapham area, and they had to travel some distance to attend religious services. The first time Mass was celebrated in Clapham since the Reformation was probably at Christmas 1847, for a group of French Sisters, the Daughters of Mary, who had came to live in Clapham Old Town where they established a residence for unemployed servant girls. The celebrant was their chaplain, Fr Thomas Sheehan.

Within a few months, two members of a small religious congregation running mission stations in more remote parts of England were offered the chaplaincy. Useful as their work of providing regular pastoral care for the scattered Catholics of Hanley Castle, Rothermere, Lantharne and Great Marlow was, it was a dead end for the future of their congregation unless they could get established in some larger centre of Catholic population. Their superior, Frederick de Held, had visited London in April 1848. A Catholic bookseller from Clapham, called John Philp, told him that a good property would shortly be coming on the market in Clapham. De Held met Bishop Wiseman, the pro-vicar apostolic for the London region, and outlined to him his hopes for moving his brethren to London. Wiseman was enthusiastic and immediately offered him the chaplaincy to the Daughters of Mary, which would provide living accommodation for two priests. With his *confrère*, Louis de Buggenoms, de Held took up residence in St Anne's House, Clapham Old Town, in June 1848. The Redemptorists had arrived.

In search of a home

The cramped accommodation in the Sisters' house was not suitable for a religious community, especially for one that was determined to add a church, no matter how small, to the basic living accommodation. Various properties were looked at, but the most attractive one seemed to be the former home of Lord Teignmouth, now divided into two residences and with a large garden. It had, besides, a large room that could serve as a chapel until it was feasible to build a church. After Teignmouth's death, the house had been purchased by Sir William Pearson, a physician. The only problem was the price. The asking price was £4,000, with £1,000 to be paid directly, and the remainder as a mortgage over seven years. It would strain the resources of a relatively poor community, but de Held took the risk and received the keys on 31 July 1848, just in time to allow the room designated as a chapel to be set up for the first Mass on the feast of St Alphonsus Liguori, founder of the Redemptorists, on 2 August. In the event, the morning Mass was celebrated by Mgr George Talbot, a well-known English convert priest who served as chamberlain to Pope Pius IX, while Wiseman officiated and preached at vespers in the evening.

Nicholas Cardinal Wiseman, Archbishop of Westminster

For a contributor to the Catholic *Rambler* magazine (1849), there was something of a sense of exultation as he conjured up every aspect of Catholic practice most anathema to Evangelicals:

> The room in Lord Teignmouth's house at Clapham (where the Bible Society was first planned) is now a Catholic chapel. Where Wilberforce and Thornton, Zachary McAuley and Greville Sharpe gossiped, dined, devised schemes for the abolition of slavery, articles for the Christian Observer and machinery for scattering printed Bibles all over the world – there now kneels a cowled monk, adoring the Blessed Sacrament of the altar, invoking Mary's intercession and praying for the souls in purgatory – such are the mutations in human things.

The available accommodation in the house was soon filled with Redemptorists. The temporary chapel could accommodate 200 people. On Sundays and holydays, Mass was celebrated at 7, 9 and 11 am, with an evening service at 7 pm and devotions for children at 4 pm. Since most of the members of the community were still struggling with English, there was no question of preaching parish missions, but a number of retreats to clergy and Sisters were given. In December 1848, the first Redemptorist mission in England was preached at St George's, Southwark.

The Clapham community at the end of 1848 consisted of Fathers de Held (Austrian), Patrack (Austrian), de Buggenoms (Belgian), Theunis (Belgian), Petcherine (Russian), Hecker (American), three professed Brothers and a Brother novice. There was a total of twenty-two Redemptorists in England between Clapham and the small mission stations. In addition to their own chapel, they were asked to take charge of the German Chapel near Blackfriars Bridge that had been designated as a centre for German-speaking Catholics in London. This was not an unreasonable request, given that several of the priests in the community were either native German speakers or native speakers of Flemish or Dutch, who would have been reasonably at ease with German. The chapel also attracted the Irish poor fleeing from the famine that had ravaged their country for the previous three years. There was an early morning Low Mass with a sung High Mass and sermon in German later in the morning. In the afternoon, there was a confraternity service.

The numbers of Irish flocking to Clapham made a larger church imperative. A year to the day after the first public Mass, the foundation stone of the new church was laid. It was calculated that there were about 212 Catholics in Clapham itself, with more than 150 scattered in Stockwell, Brixton and Tooting, who were ministered to by the Redemptorists. The architect chosen for the building was a young Catholic called William Wardell, a disciple of Augustus Welby Pugin, the apostle of the Gothic Revival. The sum of £7,000 was agreed with the builder as the initial estimate, but, inevitably, the price soared. Some money came in through collections, but the greatest help came from two benefactors, Mrs Petre, a widowed member of an old recusant family who eventually joined the Sisters of Notre Dame, and Fr Edward Douglas, a Scotsman recently professed as a Redemptorist, who undertook to defray the entire cost from his not inconsiderable personal fortune. We will learn more about the personalities of both Wardell and Douglas in due time.

Redemptorist superiors meeting in Bischenberg in Alsace in 1850 were determined to restructure the somewhat ramshackle and over-extended presence of their Congregation in England. All the small mission stations, including the German

A Catholic Church for Clapham

Chapel, were to be abandoned, and for the future, only foundations that offered the possibility of living the traditional way of life dictated by the Redemptorist Rule and of engaging in the Congregation's chosen apostolate of parish missions were to be accepted. St Mary's, Clapham was designated as such a house, with Fr de Held as its canonical superior (rector) and with a regular community assigned to it.

Opening the Church

Between the laying of the church's foundation stone in 1849 and its official opening in May 1851, a momentous change had taken place in the fortunes of the English Catholic Church. By a papal bull, *Universalis Ecclesiae*, issued in September, 1850, Pope Pius IX restored the Catholic hierarchy to England, with one metropolitan archbishop in Westminster and twelve suffragan bishops. The following day, Nicholas Wiseman was appointed archbishop of Westminster and elevated to the rank of cardinal. A week later, he addressed his first pastoral letter to the Catholics of England, titling it *From out the Flaminian Gate*, from the name of the city gate in Rome that opened on to the Via Flaminia leading northwards.

Wiseman might have been forgiven a certain triumphalism in celebrating the return of the English episcopate but many readers, especially Anglicans, found the tone of his letter bombastic. Among them was the prime minister, Lord John Russell, who described the restoration of the hierarchy as an act of "papal aggression" and introduced an *Ecclesiastical Titles Bill*, forbidding the use of any of the traditional sees as part of an episcopal title by another church. It is even reported that Queen Victoria asked in exasperation: "Am I Queen of England or am I not?"

In Wiseman's defence, it might be remembered that he was a Spanish-born child of Irish parents who had spent most of his life on the European mainland, and he probably underestimated the effect of the flamboyant language of his pastoral letter. His subsequent *Appeal to the People of England on the Catholic Hierarchy* was more conciliatory in tone. Russell had raised the spectre of the Catholic bishops demanding the restoration of churches and other property they had lost during the Reformation. Wiseman insisted this was not the case. The allegation that his title as Archbishop of Westminster implied a claim on the Abbey was mistaken:

> Close under the Abbey of Westminster there lie concealed labyrinths of lanes and courts, and alleys and slums, nests of ignorance, vice, depravity and crime, as well as squalor, wretchedness, and disease; whose atmosphere is typhus, whose ventilation is cholera; in which swarms a huge and almost countless population

… This is the part of Westminster which alone I covet, and which I shall be glad to visit, as a blessed pasture in which sheep of Holy Church are to be tended, in which a Bishop's godly work has to be done, of consoling; converting and preserving.

It was against this uneasy background that the solemn opening of St Mary's was set for 14 May 1851. Sensing that there might be trouble, de Held took the precaution of blessing the church at 5.30 in the morning, with only the Redemptorist community taking part. The liturgical procession around the outside of the building while chanting psalms and sprinkling holy water was done as unobtrusively as possible. At 10.30, the cardinal appeared. According to the account of the event in the house chronicles:

> A large crowd which was assembled in the street, saluted his Eminence with marks of ill-will, for the minds of the people at this time were excited by what they called 'the papal aggression' in establishing the Catholic hierarchy in England but the faithful Catholic Irish people greeted his Eminence with loud and enthusiastic cheers.

Twenty Redemptorists, sixty visiting priests and four bishops attended the Mass and remained for dinner. There was another hostile demonstration as they went from the church to lunch, but the police dispersed the demonstrators. The day concluded with the celebration of solemn vespers at 5 pm.

Oldest Picture of St Mary's before the transept and present monastery were built

Opposition to the Redemptorists was not merely confined to the handful of demonstrators at the church's opening. A number of publications warned the unsuspecting of the errors of the Redemptorists. One of them, *Romanism in England Exposed: The Redemptorist Fathers of St Mary's Convent, Park Road, Clapham* (1851) took the form of a series of letters by Charles Hastings Collette, and attacked the Redemptorists on many grounds, from their promotion of devotion to the scapulars to alleged errors in the theology of St Alphonsus. A more concerted attack on Alphonsus's moral theology came in R.P. Blakney's *St Alphonsus Liguori* (1852), a collection of extracts from his moral theology, usually taken out of context.

The church was consecrated according to the solemn rite in the *Roman Ritual* on 15 October the following year, as Fr Douglas had cleared the entire debt: a church could not be consecrated until it was debt-free.

From the outset, the church was distinguished by the quality and dignity of its liturgical celebrations. A full High Mass was celebrated every Sunday, while the liturgy of major seasons like Holy Week and Christmas was carried out with as much splendour as was possible. The continental Redemptorists were accustomed to well-run public celebrations, while the convert members of the community had brought with them their Tractarian reverence for the liturgy of the Church. There was also a round of more popular devotions that appealed to the majority of the parishioners – adoration of the Blessed Sacrament on an altar decorated with flowers and candles, recitation of the rosary, devotion to Mary during the month of May, and to the Sacred Heart the following month. Many of these devotions, although common in Continental Catholicism, were largely unknown to the more staid tastes of English Catholicism of the period.

Bells and a Lawsuit

William Wardell's plan for the church included a 170-foot spire housing a complete peal of bells. It was the first, and remains the only, Catholic church in London with a full peal. The bells were hung and the spire was completed in September 1851, when Fr de Buggenoms and Brother Felician climbed to the top to set the weather vane in place. Neither architect nor community had reckoned with local opposition to the bell-ringing. Even when the only bell rung was a small one attached to the roof of the monastery to call the community or announce the Angelus, Mr Soltau, the tenant of the adjoining house, made his displeasure known.

With a full set of bells now ringing the changes, he became more irritated, and conveyed his displeasure in a letter to Fr de Held. De Held ignored the letter, but the house chronicler was forced to acknowledge that "this time, he had more show of reason on his side, as the bells were rung very frequently and often inharmoniously both by the Brothers and by unpractised bell-ringers."

Soltau brought a legal action against de Held. After an absence of two hours, the jury found him guilty and fined him forty shillings. A period of silence ensued before moderate ringing of the bells for services was attempted. Soltau took another case, and got an order totally silencing the bells. It would be more than thirteen years, when he was dead and the community had acquired his part of the house, that ringing resumed, on Christmas Day 1864. The chronicler observes, somewhat philosophically, that maybe it was a good idea to allow the bells a period of silence as too much enthusiastic ringing of them "might have damaged the tower".

The bells are but one instance of a certain Catholic triumphalism in St Mary's. Commenting on the Good Friday liturgy in 1857, the chronicler records:

> Remarkable coincidence! In the procession, the Blessed Sacrament was carried by a converted minister (Fr Coffin), the canopy was supported by four others (Frs Robinson, Livius, Howell and Watson). The sermon was preached by a convert (Fr Bridgett) and the organist and his assistant were all converts.

The signs seemed to be showing that Catholicism's "second spring" might be on its way to high summer.

2. Growing Parish, Expanding Church

The original Redemptorist Rule forbade parishes to be attached to houses of the Congregation, so that the priests of the community might be able to devote their attention exclusively to the work of parish missions.

Clapham has always kept the feast of the Holy Rosary, 7 October, as its patronal feast. A feast under the title of Our Lady of Victories was instituted in thanksgiving for the Christian victory over the Turks at the naval Battle of Lepanto in 1571. Two years later, the title was altered to Our Lady of the Rosary. Examples of churches dedicated to Our Lady of Victories include Sancta Maria delle Vittorie in Rome (where Bernini's famous statue of St Teresa of Avila is found), and Notre Dame des Victoires in Paris. It is probably the latter that has the closest link to Clapham. Both Fathers Lempfried and de Buggenoms, founders of the Falmouth mission, had celebrated Mass in it while visiting Paris.

Who were the parishioners of Clapham?

The existing records tell little about the ordinary life of the parishioners of St Mary's. The first extant baptismal register is handwritten, the ink is often faded and not always easy to read. The next one covers the period 1856 to 1870, and records that 1,310 children were baptised in fourteen years.

A separate set of registers exists for adult baptisms. These were people who were received into full communion with the Catholic Church, in most cases receiving conditional baptism. Many of the male converts spent a few days before their reception on retreat in the monastery. The converts' book includes 2,052 names between 1853 and 1908. Not all were resident in the Clapham parish, as converts were often sent to the community for instruction or retreat. Ages of the converts vary: some are children "who have reached the age of reason" (seven years of age) and are treated as what we might term "theological adults". It is reasonable to suppose that their parents had entered the Church sometime before. Occasionally, an entire family is received at the same time. Emma Underhill, with her three children aged between seven and three, were received in 1867, even though her husband remained a Protestant. Many others, judging from their age, were probably converting in order to marry a Catholic. There is little by way of comment on individual entries. Numbers vary from year to year, from two in 1853, for example, to 118 in 1898. The numbers between 1890 and 1908 are significantly higher.

Based on the surnames of the parents and godparents of the babies baptised, it might be reasonable to assume that about half of them were the children of first generation Irish immigrants. In some cases, the German or Belgian priest performing the ceremony has had to guess at the spelling of unusual Irish surnames, which further suggests the likelihood that the parents were illiterate.

Birth in the nineteenth century was often hazardous for mothers and children. Marginal notes that the child had already received an emergency baptism at home, either by a priest or a lay-person such as a midwife, are not uncommon. In danger of death, all that was required was the simple pouring of water with the baptismal formula. If the baby survived, it was eventually brought to the church, when the other baptismal ceremonies, such as the anointing, were supplied and his or her name was formally inscribed in the baptismal register. In a number of cases (all Irish), the note records Wandsworth workhouse as the place of emergency baptism. It is reasonable to conclude that a corresponding number of healthy Irish babies were born in the workhouse. Certainly, the majority of Clapham's first Irish parishioners were struggling. One marginal note tells us that a three-year-old baby was brought all the way from Islington by his Irish Catholic father, unknown to his mother, who was not a Catholic.

Relatively affluent Catholic families also brought their children for baptism. One such was young Francis Alphonsus Bourne, who was baptised by Fr Coffin on 24 March 1861, the day after his birth. The marginal note on the entry records that he was ordained priest in St Mary's in 1884 by the man who had baptised him, now bishop of Southwark. Bourne was himself consecrated coadjutor bishop of the same diocese, afterwards elevated to Westminster in 1903 and created cardinal in 1911. The future cardinal's convert father considered himself to be fortunate to live close to St Mary's where the rector, Fr Coffin, had been a leading member of the Oxford Movement, and where the large number of priests meant that the liturgy could be carried out with a degree of splendour available in few London churches.

Much the same pattern is repeated in the marriage registers. The most common marginal note here is that a dispensation had been given for "disparity of cult", in other words, one of the spouses was not baptised. The beauty of the church probably made it an attractive place for fashionable weddings. Arthur James Plunkett of Killeen in County Meath, for example, married Elise Marie Rio whose parents lived in Clapham and belonged to the French nobility, in St Mary's. The ceremony was performed by the groom's brother, Fr William Plunkett, a member of the community. Both were sons of Lord Fingall of the Irish peerage.

Growing Parish, Expanding Church

The Reality of London Life

Nineteenth Century London was a crowded, unhealthy city

The London in which St Mary's parish was begun was the London reflected in the novels of Charles Dickens, a growing metropolis plagued by disease and crime, by smoke and fog. Clapham may have still retained a certain rural charm, enhanced by its large open Common, but the city was fast encroaching on it. It was becoming a favourite residential space for people who worked in the city and who were able to travel daily on the horse-drawn omnibus system that had been expanding since its introduction in 1831. Indeed the "man on the Clapham omnibus" became the measure for the average citizen of intelligence and common sense since it was first used in a 1903 law case. When Clapham Common tube station was opened in 1900, it was the southern-most station of the London underground.

Despite its size, London lacked an adequate sewerage system until the latter part of the nineteenth century. The Thames was more or less an open sewer that stank horribly, especially in summer time. So obnoxious was the "great stink" of 1858 that pressure was brought to bear to demand a proper system of public hygiene. It was not the smell alone that was troubling, but the disease that accompanied it. In the polluted atmosphere of London, tuberculosis was common. Cholera, a disease associated today with the poorest regions of the developing world, was endemic in nineteenth-century London. The monastery chronicle, for example, notes that there was a cholera epidemic during the summer of 1854. The German artist Settegast was painting the fresco on the arch over the sanctuary at this time. In his letters to his wife, he records how impressed he was by the care the Fathers gave to the sick whenever they were called.

In a society with no welfare state, parishes were conscious of the need to care for the poor among them. Like other Catholic parishes, St Mary's had a Society of St Elizabeth of Hungary. It was composed of women of a certain social position "for the purpose of serving God in the poor". This was done by visiting the homes of the poor, maternity cases, young widows, single women and other persons not visited by the Society of St Vincent de Paul. It also befriended unemployed servant girls, collected cast-off items of linen and clothing, mending them if possible for the use of the poor. The records of the Society in the archives from 1909 to 1939 offer us snapshots of poverty in the parish. One of the earliest cases records a widow with three children: the eldest daughter is going into domestic service, while the Vincent de Paul Brothers have offered to get the two youngest children, eight and eleven years old, into a home. In another case, a pregnant woman with a diseased arm is unable to look after her baby, so the Society finds a woman to care for it, but some months later, we learn that the child has died and the woman has lost her arm. A respectable old woman (of sixty-two!) has had to leave her situation to go into hospital. After a year, she has come out but would now like to get into the home run by the Little Sisters of the Poor. There is a hint, however, that her drinking might have contributed to the loss of her job. A widow with one child has a pension of five shillings and is unable to work due to ill-health. One of the last cases is a family with three children who are refugees from the Spanish Civil War. The Society of St Elizabeth, where possible, provided financial help, clothing and vouchers for essential foods.

A Growing Parish

By 1865, the Redemptorist houses of Clapham, Bishop Eton (Liverpool) and Limerick (Ireland) were granted independence as a province. This meant that the community was now largely, but not exclusively, composed of native English speakers. The external ministry of the community was expanding. In 1866, eleven missions and two "renewals" (short parish retreats, delivered some months after a mission had been preached), six retreats to religious and nine to other groups were preached. 120 converts were received in the course of the missions, and a further seventeen were received at Clapham. There were 150 members in the Clapham confraternity and 16,216 communions were distributed in the course of the year. This was not to be taken however as a sign to the Fathers to relax their efforts.

At the annual canonical visitation in 1866, the Provincial left the following instructions:

> Four times a year, all those parts of the district in which it is known that neglectful Catholics congregate, are to be carefully visited and the people seriously reminded of their obligation to receive the sacraments and send their children to Catholic schools.

It was recommended that the visits be paid especially before Christmas and Ash Wednesday.

The leader of the first Redemptorist community at Falmouth, Fr Louis de Buggenoms, had requested the School Sisters of Notre Dame in Bruges, whom he knew well, to establish a small foundation at Penrhyn in Wales. When the Redemptorists moved to Clapham, they appreciated the contribution of the Sisters and invited them to come to London. They founded their community in 1848 and within a few years the school was flourishing.

Growing Parish, Expanding Church

The Icon of the Mother of Perpetual Help

Our Lady of Perpetual Help Comes to Clapham

An ancient icon of Our Lady under the title of the Mother of Perpetual Help, that was long believed to have disappeared, came to light in Rome in 1865. As it had originally been venerated in a church close to where the Redemptorists' general house now stood, they asked Pope Pius IX for it to be committed to their care. He agreed, giving them the command, "Make her known to the world." The icon was installed in the Roman Redemptorist church in 1866, which had been built from the money of Fr Douglas and designed by a Scottish architect, George Wigley. It was solemnly crowned the following year by order of the Vatican. Every Redemptorist house wanted a copy for public veneration.

Clapham's copy arrived in December 1867. Bishop Grant of Southwark presided and preached at the ceremony of installation. The veiled icon was to be carried in procession, but according to the chronicler, the church was so crowded that it was only with difficulty that the procession was able to move to St Joseph's altar, which was to be its temporary home until such time as a dedicated chapel could be found for it. The celebrations continued for a further three days of prayer and sermons on the icon and its significance.

20

It was twenty years before the Lady Chapel was built. It was designed by the leading Catholic architect of the time, John Francis Bentley, a resident of the parish and a friend of many in the community. A note on him and his work in St Mary's will be found in a later chapter of this guide. The Lady Chapel was the first extension of the original church, and the cost of £2,000 was defrayed by a benefactor, Mrs Louis, in memory of her husband.

An Expanding Church

As Clapham became drawn more into the conurbation of London, the parish continued to grow. Many of the new parishioners belonged to the rising Catholic middle classes who were finding their way into the medical and legal professions and for whom Clapham was an attractive place to live. The existing church was proving too small for the regular congregations. The monastery, already an aged building when it had been bought almost fifty years previously, was in urgent need of replacement. An ambitious plan entailed building a new monastery with accommodation for clergy and laity to come on retreat, as well as for the resident community, and extending the church by adding a transept. Bentley was chosen as the architect for both.

Bentley's plans required that the community be installed in the new monastery before the old building could be demolished and the ground cleared for the transept. The monastery was completed in 1891. It is built in red brick with some allusions to medieval monastic styles in the archways and stone decorations over the windows and doorways. It has been suggested that there is a Dutch or Belgian look to it, with its ornamental chimneys and red brick. It is a functional building, with little show of extravagance, but with a subdued beauty that has been described as "arts and crafts Gothic".

Work on the new transept moved briskly. Bentley carefully imitated the lines of the existing building and, where possible, reused some features, such as the two windows that gave light to the community chapel and which can be seen on the upper left side on entering. The transept also incorporated a new altar and shrine to St Joseph, and a baptistery near the entrance, with the font enclosed behind a simple iron grille. It had been suggested to Bentley that there were sufficient funds for a new font, but the architect refused, on the grounds that his children had been baptised in the existing font. This may be forgiven as a father's sentimentality, but it also respects the deep liturgical symbolism of the font as the womb of Mother Church, as is manifest in the prayers for the blessing of baptismal water at the Easter Vigil. The same font was later moved into the sanctuary area when the church was reordered after Vatican II.

THE MAIN CORRIDOR   ST GERARD'S CORRIDOR

As the church grew in size, so too did the parish. In 1903, the Catholic population was just short of 2,000 souls, including the Sisters and children in the Notre Dame convent and school. Sunday Mass attendance stood at 1,700. If this figure is accurate and includes only parishioners and not casual worshippers at St Mary's, it suggests a practice rate of over 86 per cent. It was also estimated that 1,400 (over seventy per cent) frequented the sacraments regularly.

That same year, St Mary's lost some of its territory to the new parish of St Francis de Sales and St Gertrude in Stockwell. Despite the loss of territory, a census some years later showed that the parish still had 2,400 parishioners and showed few signs of declining: the Easter Sunday congregations in 1911 came to about 2,000.

Devotion to the Redemptorist Brother, Gerard Majella, had long been promoted in Clapham. His beatification in 1893 and canonisation in 1904 greatly increased devotion to the saint, commonly regarded as the patron of pregnant women and their unborn and newly-born children. A temporary shrine had been set up in his honour, but in 1910 it was replaced by a chapel. Designed by Osmund Bentley, its proportions and style were intended to match his father's Lady Chapel in the opposite aisle.

The First World War

War was declared on 6 August 1914. It was decided to end the school summer holidays prematurely that year in order to keep the children off the streets!

The German invasion of Belgium a few days previously had triggered Britain's declaration of war against Germany. Within a few days, the first Redemptorists began to arrive as refugees from Belgium. One of them, Brother Walter Esdaile, was a professed student of the English province who was studying in Belgium. With his companions, he had left the house of studies, as the German invasion was imminent. As a British citizen, he was in greater danger, so they parted company and he made his way to London via Ostend, with no luggage but the clothes he was wearing. By November, some sixteen Belgian Redemptorists were living in English communities. In some cases, they were accompanied by family members who had also fled. The following month, eight students arrived, who were sent to the student house at Perth, but they had to return home for military service.

Grave of Fr Bernard Kavanagh in the Commonwealth War Cemetery, Jerusalem

Within weeks of the war's beginning, volunteers for the chaplaincy service were being sought, especially among the religious orders. About a dozen English Redemptorists, and a similar number from Ireland (then still part of the United Kingdom) volunteered. Several, like Fr David Ahearne, who was awarded the Distinguished Service Order (DSO), were decorated for bravery. Two others lost their lives. Fr Bernard Kavanagh was shot by a Turkish sniper on the Mount of Olives in Jerusalem in December 1917 and Fr Charles Watson died in Baghdad the following July. Fr Watson had earlier survived for three days drifting in an open boat in the Mediterranean, when the ship in which he was travelling was torpedoed.

Throughout the war years, Masses were celebrated for the young men of the parish who had fallen in action. The first was on 2 December 1914, for John McKenzie, a former altar boy who was an officer in the London Scottish Regiment. The most public requiem was celebrated on 23 June 1917 for Major Willie Redmond, the Irish Nationalist MP, whose London home was in the parish and who had been married in the church thirty-one years earlier. His catafalque (a coffin-shaped structure used in a celebration of Requiem Mass when the body is not present) was draped with both the Union flag and the flag of the Irish Volunteers. Most of the Irish members of parliament and many others attended. At the end of the service, the "Dead March", "Let Erin Remember", and "God Save Our Gracious King" were played on the organ.

War Memorial, Sir Giles Gilbert Scott

By September 1917, the war moved closer to home with a one-hour bombing raid on London that killed fifteen people and wounded seventy-three. The early warning and all-clear were primitive in the extreme: when a raid was threatening, police constables rode through the area on their bicycles blowing their whistles, while the all-clear was given by scouts driven through the area and blowing two notes on a bugle!

To commemorate the dead of the parish, a War Memorial Cross designed by Sir Giles Gilbert Scott, a leading Catholic architect, was dedicated in December 1920.

Still expanding

The growth of the parish showed no signs of diminishing. Since additional Sunday Masses did not solve the problem, a further extension to the church seemed inevitable. The logical thing would have been to match the south transept by building another on the opposite side, but the closeness of the houses on the front of the Common made this impossible. Two properties were acquired next door to the church on Clapham Park Road, and the architect George Bernard Cox of Birmingham drew up a plan to extend St Gerard's chapel by adding another aisle.

Cox's plans for the church included the removal of the organ and choir from the gallery over the main door and their relocation in the chapel of St Alphonsus near the sanctuary. A place would then have to be found for a new chapel of St Alphonsus. It was decided to relocate it near the entrance under the tower. The work was to be undertaken by Holloway Brothers for £5,000. Work began in March 1929 and proceeded so rapidly that by the following March Cardinal Bourne, a former parishioner and now archbishop of Westminster, was able to come to bless the new extension.

War Again

By the late 1930s, the monastery chronicler noted that war once more seemed inevitable. As early as March 1938, the cellars were "being cleaned and whitewashed with a view to making them anti-gas shelters (so much talk of 'war')", and a visiting Redemptorist passing through Germany reported the change of mood in that country. A Canadian Redemptorist, Bishop Gerald Murray, for example, told of how, when he had celebrated Mass in Cologne cathedral and had innocently asked a priest how things were in Germany, he was taken aside and warned not to ask questions like that again, as both of them could easily find themselves in a concentration camp. At the end of August 1939, the rector requested all visiting Redemptorists staying in the house to return to their home provinces. A week later, war was declared.

Once again, there was a request for chaplains for the forces. The local schools were evacuated and some of the Redemptorists were asked to accompany the children and teachers to the remote country districts where they were billeted, and where priests were in short supply. The community acquired its first radio to follow the war news and receive whatever public announcements were made.

In June 1940, the first chaplain to have served in Dunkirk briefly visited the community, still wearing battle dress, and gave a vivid account of his escape from France. "He directed a convoy personally on one occasion," the chronicler recorded, "escaping narrowly from being ambushed by enemy tanks, enduring days of unremitting bombing at the place of embarkation. All his kit was left or was destroyed."

The mood in the country was so bleak that the rector gave instructions as to what was to be done in the event of a civil evacuation. The Blessed Sacrament, in both church and community oratory, was to be consumed, and the holy oils distributed among the Fathers. If possible, each priest was to take a chalice. The church and monastery were to be handed over to the military, if required. Everyone was to keep a small suitcase ready and when the time came, each would be given a sum of money. If at all possible, everyone was to make his way to Hawkstone, the house of studies. As this was a remote house in Shropshire with a farm attached, it was probably the safest place available.

Despite the hardship and the frequent air raids, during which much time was spent in the cellars, morale in both parish and community remained high. "Our people are wonderfully brave," noted the chronicler, "and in spite of sleepless nights and danger by day, the church has been well attended." Throughout the war, Clapham

Alphonsus Liguori, Founder of the Redemptorists

was a place for spiritual and human renewal for chaplains, no matter what army they served. Each month, it offered a retreat day to as many British chaplains as were free to avail of it.

The liturgy continued to be celebrated to a very high standard. A young parishioner with an Oxford degree in music, George Malcolm, had been appointed director of the choir and organist before the war. When he was called up, he was appointed head of an RAF band based in London. Somehow, he managed to arrange his leave to coincide with the liturgical needs of Clapham, especially at Holy Week and Christmas. From 1944 until 1949, Archbishop Amigo of Southwark came to Clapham to consecrate the holy oils on Maundy Thursday, as St George's, his cathedral, had been severely damaged in a bombing raid. After the war, George Malcolm found a full-time post as director of music at Westminster Cathedral and as his career developed, he became well known for his work in early music and recordings, especially with the harpsichord.

By Easter, 1945 the end was in sight as the blackout ended and Germany surrendered. A lasting memorial of the war in St Mary's was the weekly novena in honour of Our Lady of Perpetual Help. It had been introduced to the Redemptorist church in Belfast by an American Redemptorist chaplain in 1942 and proved to be an outstanding success in those dark days. The provincial, Fr John Charlton, asked for it to be introduced in all the houses of the province in thanksgiving for their protection during the war.

An extraordinary act of fraternal kindness and reconciliation was performed by the English province immediately after the war. Fr Charlton opened up negotiations with the Allied Control Commission to obtain permission for the students of the German province to come to England to continue their studies. Many of these young men had been conscripted into the Wehrmacht during the war and were returning to religious life in very difficult conditions. The first group of thirteen, with their teachers of theology, arrived in September 1947 and were brought to Hawkstone, where they lived, prayed, studied and played in community alongside their English Brothers.

A Hundred Years and Changing

In June 1948, the community celebrated its centenary. In preparation for it, some work of maintenance and restoration of the church took place under the direction of Sir Giles Gilbert Scott. It included the restoration of some windows in the Lady Chapel that had been shattered during war-time bombing. The community chapel also received attention. The Gothic artists, Ninian Comper and his son Sebastian, supervised the restoration of Bentley's reredos, and depicted on it the three Redemptorist saints, Alphonsus, Clement and Gerard, two of whom (Clement and Gerard) had been canonised since Bentley's time. Bentley's decorated ceiling was left in its original condition but carefully cleaned.

In the early 1950s, the parish seemed to be in a flourishing state. According to the annual returns for the years 1952 to 1955, baptisms outnumbered funerals (796 to 142) and marriages in which both parties were Catholic numbered 207, with a further eighty-nine mixed marriages. There are no figures for Sunday Mass attendance, and the number of communions distributed (255,000) is only a very rough indicator, since it includes daily Masses and other special occasions.

The national background of parishioners was also changing. A quick survey of the baptismal register for the period 1949–1955 suggests that, while the English and Irish names that had figured in the earlier registers still remained to the fore, there was now a substantial number of Italian and Eastern European, and particularly, Polish names – nearly fifteen per cent of the total. Many of these baptisms seem to have been done by a chaplain to the Polish community, so it is not always clear whether the family was resident in St Mary's parish or not. It represents, however, an increasing diversity within the Catholic Church in England.

Minor changes were altering the ordinary rhythms of Catholic life. When fasting from midnight was a condition for the reception of Holy Communion, most communicants attended early morning Masses. Changes in the eucharistic fasting regulations in 1958 reduced the fast to three hours (eventually to one). Sunday Mass times were hourly, from 7 am until the High Mass at 11 am: there was one more at 12.15 pm and the final Mass of the day at 5.30 pm. On weekdays, Mass was at 6.30 am, 7 am, 7.30 am, 8.45 am and 9.30 am. The Second Vatican Council, beginning in 1962, introduced even greater changes in the manner in which Mass was celebrated. The most important change was a shift from the exclusive use of Latin to the language of the people. The unintended result was that many aspects of life in St Mary's changed almost overnight, including change in a musical tradition that had been in place since the church was opened.

The Council also brought about changes in the relationship with other Christian denominations. The rector, Fr Anthony Freeman, was invited to preach at Holy Trinity Church on the Common in November 1965 and the annual celebration during the week of prayer for the unity of Christians becomes a fixed point in the churches' year. There was much excitement when the BBC asked St Mary's to host a service to be recorded in advance. In February 1966, Fr Freeman presided at a service at which the preacher was the distinguished German Redemptorist theologian, Fr Bernard Häring. It was broadcast a month later to the delight of the community.

Who are our parishioners?

A detailed study of social change in the parish of St Mary is well beyond the limits of this guide. However, a brief survey of the baptismal registers provides a general impression of the parents who brought their babies for baptism in the church. Several words of caution are essential, however. First of all, it is not always possible to tell the ethnic background of a person from how they spell their name. Secondly, names that look or sound traditionally British or Irish may be borne by people of, say, Canadian, Australian or Caribbean origin, just as people with Spanish or Portuguese-sounding names might just as likely come from Cape Verde or Goa in India.

With these reservations in mind, a probe of the baptismal registers indicates that St Mary's in the last quarter of the twentieth century became less homogenous than it had been even twenty years previously. While English and Irish names still accounted for sixty per cent of baptisms in 1977 and Eastern Europeans for almost seven per cent, more than ten per cent of the names were now of African origin. Another probe in the opening years of the twenty-first century (2004), showed firstly that the number of baptisms had declined (seventy-four against one hundred and thirty-two or fifty-six per cent). Although British and Irish names remained to the fore, the percentage had declined (fifty-three per cent), while the percentage of African names had risen sharply (twenty-five per cent).

Change of that sort was to be the norm for the rest of the twentieth century and into the first two decades of the twenty-first. It has been estimated that the members of St Mary's parish have about forty languages, either as native speakers or having learned them through their parents.

Major Church Restoration

The changes introduced into the celebration of the liturgy, such as greater participation of the laity, prayers and readings in the language of the people and indeed, a fresh understanding of the significance and importance of the celebration of the Eucharist in the life of the parish, made a thorough renewal of the church, especially of the sanctuary area, imperative.

Work was begun in September 1984 and continued until the following June. It was so intensive that the church could only be used at weekends, and even then with some inconvenience. Weekday Masses and other services were held in the large parlour of the monastery. While not ideal, it had some benefits, especially in deepening the relationship between priests and people.

The first major task entailed the removal of the altar rails separating the sanctuary from the nave to enlarge the sanctuary area. A permanent free-standing altar was installed to replace the temporary altar that had been in place since the introduction of the revised rite of Mass in the late 1960s. It is in keeping with the style of the church, as it was taken from the chapel of St Alphonsus. Modifications to the pulpit enabled it to be used as the ambo, or place for the proclamation of the word of God from scripture during the liturgy.

The sanctuary furnishings were completed by the transfer of the baptismal font from the baptistery at the rear of the transept. One of the theological results of the Second Vatican Council was the recognition of the sacrament of baptism as the entry of every believer into the depths of the mystery of Christ and with it a share in Christ's priesthood. The traditional place of the baptistery, close to the entrance to the church, stressed its place as a *liminal* sacrament, a "rite of the threshold", at which usually only members of the baby's family were present. Its present position enables baptism to be celebrated in a more communal context in the presence of the whole parish community. The ideal time for this is the Easter Vigil, or, as often happens, during the celebration of a Sunday liturgy. The font is the one originally designed for the church by Wardell, but carefully cleaned and restored. To create space for the font, the statue of Our Lady in its shrine had to be raised somewhat. Finally, as an aid to security, the grille separating the choir and organ area and sanctuary was removed and placed at the top of the aisle near the transept. This allowed the transept to be closed off from the rest of the church as a matter of security while still permitting the faithful to pray in the presence of the Blessed Sacrament.

3. The Redemptorists

St Mary's Church and monastery belongs to a community of Redemptorist priests and Brothers. The name 'Redemptorists' is taken from their official Latin title, *Congregatio Sanctissimi Redemptoris*, the Congregation of the Most Holy Redeemer. It is abbreviated to C.Ss.R, which the members normally use after their names. Later in this chapter, we shall consider some of the individuals who shaped that story, but let us begin with a brief look at the history of the Redemptorists.

Who are the Redemptorists?

The Redemptorists are a Congregation of priests and Brothers who live in community, bound by the traditional three vows of religion (poverty, chastity and obedience) and an additional vow of perseverance, that commits them to the Congregation until death. They were founded on 9 November 1732 in a small town called Scala, high above the beautiful coast of Amalfi, by a young priest from Naples called Alphonsus Maria de Liguori (1696–1787). Born into the minor nobility of the Kingdom of Naples, Alphonsus had begun a precocious but highly successful early career at the bar. A disastrous law case, involving some sharp practice on the part of his opponents, brought him to reconsider his future in the courts. To the horror of his ambitious father, he applied to become a priest in the diocese of Naples. Ordained at the age of thirty and contrary to the hopes of his family that he would cultivate an ecclesiastical career that would lead to a mitre, Alphonsus devoted himself instead to ministry among the poorest – the workers of the city and its suburbs, the shepherds and goatherds in the mountains to the south.

There was no shortage of priests in eighteenth-century Naples. Quite the contrary, there were too many priests with little to do by way of pastoral work. The situation was different in the hinterland. Shocked by the spiritual ignorance and pastoral neglect he found in the mountain villages, Alphonsus resolved, with a small group of like-minded companions, to minister for them and other "most abandoned souls". The beginnings of the Congregation were enthusiastic, but within a few months, all but one of his first companions had abandoned him. The one remaining was a layman called Vito Curzio, the first lay Brother of the Congregation. Painfully, Alphonsus and Vito picked up the threads of what had begun with such enthusiasm.

31

The Redemptorists

St Clement Hofbauer "second founder" of the Redemptorists

Alphonsus's way of reaching people with the good news of the Gospel was through a method known as the "parish mission". This was an intensive course of instruction on the basic teachings of the Church with a call to radical conversion and recommitment, along with the celebration of the sacraments. Emerging in seventeenth-century France under the influence of Church reformers like Vincent de Paul, parish missions were instruments of mass evangelisation. The parish mission arrived in Italy not long after this, and among its principal proponents, were the Jesuits of the Kingdom of Naples. The members of Alphonsus's community combined periods of intense itinerant preaching from parish to parish, when the weather and the agricultural calendar made it feasible, with time devoted to prayer and study in the solitude of the community house.

For more than fifty years until his death, Alphonsus struggled for the survival of his Congregation with a government that respected religion, but did not want any more religious Orders, much less Orders that looked beyond the borders of the Kingdom of Naples to the authority of Rome. By a tragic turn of events, Alphonsus, now an infirm old man, deaf and almost blind, ended up formally excluded by the pope from the Congregation he had founded. It looked like the end of a dream, except for a curious development. Two young Bohemian pilgrims to Rome, Clement Hofbauer and Thadeus Hübl, found themselves one morning hearing Mass in the small church of a religious congregation of which they had never heard. Within a short time, they had applied to join it, were received, professed, ordained and sent back home with the mission to found a house of the Congregation somewhere within the boundaries of the Austrian Empire.

By 1787, Clement had established a vibrant community in Warsaw. Twenty years later, it was swept away by the Napoleonic wars. A small group of students and novices under the leadership of a Frenchman called Joseph Passerat spent years wandering and living in temporary accommodation. Clement eventually made his way to Vienna where he became a popular preacher, attracting young artists and intellectuals. All the time, he fought to save his Congregation. He was granted royal permission to found a community in Vienna. When the imperial decree of authorisation arrived in 1820, Clement was already dead and the decree was laid on his coffin.

And so to England

The pent-up energy of the preceding years of struggle finally found release as the Redemptorists spread throughout Europe with extraordinary rapidity. At the time of Hofbauer's death, there was but a single community of twenty-seven members north of the Alps, living in a dilapidated former Carthusian monastery at Valsainte in

Switzerland. One professed Redemptorist lived in Vienna as Hofbauer's companion. A handful of others lived in twos and threes in the principality of Walachia and in Poland. During the next thirty years, the Redemptorists spread rapidly: to Alsace in 1829, Belgium in 1831, to the United States to care for German emigrants in 1832, then to Holland 1836. In the twenty-eight years between the death of Clement and the foundation of Clapham, the Congregation had grown to nearly 500 priests and Brothers, with over 120 students and novices.

During a stay in Belgium in 1837, Dr Augustine Baines, vicar apostolic of the Western District, had occasion to meet the Redemptorist provincial superior, Frederick de Held. Conscious of the shortage of priests in his district, and especially in Wales, Baines pleaded with de Held for help but without success, since the number of active Redemptorists was still low and they were overwhelmed by the demand for parish mission work. Five years later, another appeal came, this time from Scotland. In response, de Held went to see the situation first hand. It was clear, however, that Scotland was out of the question, but this time, de Held took the initiative. He returned Bishop Baines's visit: the outcome of their meeting was an agreement to accept a small mission in Falmouth in Cornwall. Three Redemptorists, Frs Louis de Buggenoms, Auguste Lempfried and Brother Felician Dubucquoi, arrived in June 1843.

Fr Louis de Buggenoms : Redemptorist Pioneer in Britain

It was hardly an auspicious beginning. Only de Buggenoms spoke English with relative fluency and the Redemptorists were shocked by the poverty of the mission. They were forced to accept responsibility for a geographically extensive pastoral area where only seven or eight people attended Sunday Mass. They set out to improve the standard of what was on offer. Catholics were virtually unknown in Cornwall, and for a short time, the curious flocked to the little chapel. De Buggenoms did his best to raise funds for the new mission among the old Catholic recusant families, and names like Lord Stourton, Sir Edward Vavasour and the Petre family figure among his benefactors. His sheer persistence paid off, and the congregation had grown to 170 in little over a year. Fr De Buggenoms realised that a school was essential, and he persuaded the Sisters of Notre Dame de Namur he had known in Belgium, to make a foundation at nearby Penryn.

Another mission, at Hanley Castle in Worcestershire, was accepted the following year and looked more promising. A Catholic landlord, Thomas Hornyold, had built a church and residence. Another church in Great Marlow, Buckinghamshire, built by a convert Member of Parliament, Charles Scott Murray, was accepted in 1846. With pastoral responsibility for mission stations, there was little possibility of attempting their Congregation's tradition of parish mission preaching which some

Frederick de Held: Founder of Clapham

of the English bishops hoped they might take up. When de Held had finished his term as provincial superior in Belgium, he was sent to take over at Hanley Castle. He never arrived, as a visit to London concluded with the decision to install a community in Clapham.

A meeting of superiors in 1859 at Bischenberg, near Strasbourg, decreed that small mission stations should be abandoned and that any future foundations should aim to be in the style of the relatively large communities envisaged by the Rule, composed of twelve priests and seven brothers. With the establishment of communities at Bishop Eton (Liverpool) in 1851 and Limerick (Ireland) in 1853 without pastoral responsibility for Mass stations, that now seemed a reality. It was decided to withdraw from Falmouth, Hanley Castle and Great Marlow and to concentrate resources on Clapham, Bishop Eton and Limerick, eventually including Kinnoull in Perth. The three houses formed part of the Anglo–Dutch province from 1855 until ten years later, when they became the nucleus of an independent province.

An Austrian, a Belgian, a Russian, and an American

Clapham was constituted as a formal community, that is, a *collegium* under a rector, in 1850. The rector, Frederick de Held, was an Austrian. With him, there were five priests – a Belgian, Louis de Buggenoms, Vladimir Petcherine, a Russian, two Austrians, Wenceslaus Haklik and Germanus Kittel, a recently ordained American called Isaac Hecker, and three Belgian Brothers (Francis Funduer, Louis Dubois and Felician Dubucquoi), two novice Brothers (James Murclaer and Joseph Burowsky), and a postulant called Paul Faber.

De Held was the eldest at fifty-one. He was also the living link with Clement Hofbauer, the second founder of the Congregation. As a student, he had been a member of Clement's circle of young intellectuals and artists. He had carried Clement's coffin at his funeral and he entered the Congregation on the strength of the imperial decree of authorisation. He was professed in 1821 and ordained priest two years later. It was he who agreed to the first Redemptorist mission in England and eventually planned the Clapham house, so he can lay claim to being the founder of the London province. As provincial of Belgium from 1841 until 1847, the recent American foundation also came under his jurisdiction and he visited the American houses in 1845. De Held's early association with Clement gave him a significant role in the congregation and for much of his life, he was superior and advisor. He died in Holland in 1881.

When Louis de Buggenoms was appointed superior to the new English mission, he was twenty-seven years of age and a priest for just a few months. He had the advantage of good spoken English. De Buggenoms ministered in England until he was appointed superior of the new foundation in Limerick in 1853. He remained there for several years, and was instrumental in gathering candidates for the first convent of Redemptoristine Sisters in Dublin which opened in 1859. That same year, he went to the West Indies where he remained until 1874. He died in Brussels in 1882.

Vladimir Petcherine was the most colourful and talented of the early Redemptorists. Born near Kiev in the Ukraine in 1807, his intellectual prowess brought him to the universities of St Petersburg and Moscow. Having completed a doctorate in 1835, he was appointed professor of Greek philology at the University of Moscow. Tiring of the tightly controlled world of Tsarist Russia, Petcherine arranged to take sabbatical leave to travel outside Russia. While in Belgium in 1838, he came under the influence of a Redemptorist and converted to Roman Catholicism. He entered the Redemptorist novitiate in 1840 and, after a short course of theology, was ordained priest. He was sent to the Falmouth foundation and then to Clapham. He was the first Redemptorist to work in Ireland, having given a retreat to Sisters immediately prior to the first Limerick mission in 1851. His passionate nature, allied to a natural sympathy for the underdog, led to conflict in Ireland, including a trial on a charge of bible-burning, of which he was acquitted. It set him on a collision course with his superiors however. He left the Redemptorists in 1861, with the intention of entering a contemplative community. Having tried in turn the Carthusians and the Cistercians, he attempted to return to the Redemptorists. His superiors were adamant that they would not have him back. He spent the next twenty-four years working as a hospital chaplain in Dublin. In 1991, his remains were reburied in the Redemptorist plot in Dublin.

The only native speaker of English among them was the young American, Isaac Hecker. Hecker was born in New York in 1819, the child of German emigrants. He became a Catholic in 1844 and, shortly afterwards, entered the Redemptorists. He was sent to make his novitiate in St Trond in Belgium where he was professed in 1846. Theological studies followed in Holland, but the young man's health was fragile and he spent the last months of his course reading privately in Clapham, where he was eventually ordained by Cardinal Wiseman in 1849. He remained in Clapham for a few years but he was sent back to America in 1851. Like Petcherine, Hecker was not destined to remain in the Redemptorists. With some of his native-born American brethren, he felt that the Redemptorists in America should be addressing themselves to Americans, rather than simply attending to the spiritual needs of the German emigrant population. As a result of a misunderstanding with his Roman superiors, Hecker was forcibly dispensed from his vows. He founded an independent religious community, the Society of St Paul, in 1858.

Even as the number of native English speakers in the community increased, life in a multinational community was not without its tensions. The visitation "recesses", or points of observance requiring attention, occasionally drew attention to the obligation to speak only English in the house, and that "Fathers and Brothers will scrupulously take care not to annoy *confrères* ... about their nationality, even jocosely". There was also the question of the social division between the better educated priests and the Brothers who looked after the practical matters of the house such as cooking and cleaning. Another visitation recess reminds the Fathers to remember "that the brothers are their brothers and they will strive to make themselves loved by them rather than feared ... they will refrain from imposing on them any more than is necessary".

The First Generation

When they arrived in Falmouth, the Redemptorists were a virtually unknown religious congregation of foreigners. Within a few years of their arrival, they were attracting talented young men, many of whom were converts from the Oxford Movement. It is not easy to explain the attraction. In part, it is probably due to the impact of the writings of their founder, Alphonsus Liguori, that were beginning to become known. Newman's entry to the Catholic Church was facilitated by Charles Russell, a young professor in Maynooth College who recommended him to read Alphonsus' *Glories of Mary* as a way of understanding what the Oxford man regarded as the excesses of Catholic devotional life. The house at Clapham became a popular venue for retreats for young men, either pondering the decision to enter the Catholic Church or whether or not to pursue a religious vocation. Redemptorist community life was regarded as austere and may have appealed to idealistic young men. Finally there was the Redemptorist apostolate of parish missions that was beginning to have remarkable success in its outreach to urban and rural parishes alike.

The first generation of Redemptorists in Britain were a varied group of men. They included William Plunkett, an Irish aristocrat and army officer, John Furniss and Francis Weld, of old English Catholic or "recusant" origin, converts like Thomas Livius or working class men like Joachim Kelly who entered the Brotherhood. The four whose portraits follow here may not be typical but they illustrate the reach of the first generation of Redemptorists.

The Scottish Millionaire

Edward Douglas (1819–98) was born into a wealthy and aristocratic Scottish family. Edward's father died when he was eleven years of age. As an only child, he inherited the sizeable fortune that had come to his father from his Queensbury relatives. Edward was educated at Eton and Christ Church, Oxford. John Henry Newman, a don of Oriel College, was the most controversial figure in the university at the time. The series of theological *Tracts for the Times* he had inspired began to appear in 1833. By the time of the appearance of the final Tract 90, *Remarks on Certain Passages in the Thirty Nine Articles*, which argued that the Anglican *Articles of Religion* could be interpreted in a way that was agreeable with Catholic doctrine, Edward Douglas had already left the university, having failed his final degree examinations.

Fr Edward Douglas in old age

Douglas had been a devout young man but he had avoided the Tractarian debates. This position changed with the debate that raged around Tract 90, and Douglas became convinced that his future lay in the Church of Rome, and towards the end of 1841, he travelled to Italy with a friend, Charles Scott Murray, who would later bring the Redemptorists to Great Marlow. While attending a ceremony at St Peter's Basilica, Scott Murray had put his umbrella into one of the confessionals for safety. When they returned to retrieve it after the ceremony, the confessional was locked. Murray had to leave Rome quickly, so Douglas undertook to recover the lost umbrella. His search led him to a Carmelite friary near St Peter's, where a friendship with a young priest ensued. Douglas decided to be received into the Catholic Church almost immediately, and he was baptised conditionally in 1842, some three years ahead of Newman.

His mother was horrified by the news, and she dispatched an Anglican clergyman to Rome in an attempt to reconvert him but without success. From the time of his conversion, Douglas had entertained the possibility of becoming a priest. It was a step he was reluctant to take, however, for fear of the additional pain it might cause his mother. Relations between mother and son were restored, and by June 1848, Douglas was ordained in Italy. Shortly after his ordination, he made a pilgrimage to the tomb of St Alphonsus at Pagani, south of Naples, to pray for guidance in deciding his future ministry as a priest. By the end of the year, he was in the Redemptorist novitiate at St Trond in Belgium, where he made his vows on the feast of the Immaculate Conception 1849. He was the first Briton to be professed in the congregation.

Robert Aston Coffin as Bishop of Southwark
Courtesy of Archdiocesan Archives, Southwark

By the end of February 1850, Fr Douglas returned to England as a member of the newly-founded Clapham community. Thanks to his personal wealth, he was able to clear the outstanding debt on the church. He was part of the first Redemptorist community in Mount St Alphonsus, Limerick, where, it was hoped, he might again dip into his ample money to cover the cost of building the church and monastery. His superiors had other plans, however. The Redemptorists had been ordered by the Pope to transfer the residence of their general from Pagani, near Naples, to Rome, and a suitable house was needed for the purpose. Douglas again obliged, and built the church and monastery on the Via Merulana. He would later cover the cost of the foundations at Perth in his native Scotland and at Cortona in Italy.

A man of Douglas's background was bound to attract attention in Rome. His opinion in matters relating to Britain, and especially Scotland, was sought by the Holy See. He became a point of reference for English visitors to Rome, especially converts trying to work through the final stages of their entry to the Catholic Church. He served his Congregation as a general councillor, as provincial of the Roman province and as rector of the house on the Via Merulana. When the Army of Italian Reunification invaded Rome in 1870 and confiscated much church-owned property, Douglas saved the house by running up the Union Flag over it and claiming it as British property. Edward Douglas died in Rome in 1898.

The Oxford Vicar

Robert Aston Coffin (1819–85) was the eldest of five children of a prosperous merchant family in Brighton. As a child, he had wondered whether he should become an opera singer or a bishop, but decided the matter by going on to read theology at Oxford. After ordination in 1843, he was appointed vicar of St Mary Magdalene's, one of the more fashionable churches in Oxford. It was inevitable that Coffin should become embroiled in the theological debates of Oxford at the time, and the young vicar was soon drawn into Newman's circle.

Coffin's moment of crisis came when he was summoned to the bedside of a dying parishioner. He ministered to her according to the rites of the *Book of Common Prayer* but, as he began the words of absolution, the woman interrupted him: "I believe you don't know whether you are a priest or not." In consternation, Coffin asked her what she meant, and when he discovered she believed that the true Christian priesthood only existed in the Catholic Church, he went to fetch the Catholic priest for her who heard her confession before she died.

Oxford gossip about the incident did nothing to enhance Coffin's standing or to allay his doubts about the nature of the Church of England. Newman had, by this time, withdrawn to the village of Littlemore to escape the storm following the publication of Tract 90 and he entered the Roman Catholic Church in October 1845. Coffin continued to hesitate, but was received in December. After much hesitation about which religious community to join, Newman decided to establish a branch of the Oratory of St Philip Neri, especially for converts. He assembled a group of six prospective novices, including Coffin, in Rome in early 1847. Coffin was ordained priest later that year. After their novitiate, they returned to England and established their community at Maryvale, near Birmingham. Coffin's heart was not in the Oratory, and tensions were beginning to show between himself and Newman. By 1851, Coffin had left the Oratory for the Redemptorist novitiate in Belgium, where he was professed in February 1852.

Coffin's talents and social contacts with both old recusant families and many of the new Oxford converts marked him out for leadership in the English Church. When the Anglo–Dutch province divided in 1865, he was appointed provincial of the London province, which included the houses in Ireland. He held that office until he was nominated bishop of Southwark in 1882. His episcopate lasted a mere three years. He died in April 1885 in the Redemptorist house of studies at Teignmouth in Devon that he had founded and where he is buried.

The Cambridge Scholar

Thomas Edward Bridgett (1829–99) was the youngest of the first group of Englishmen to enter the Redemptorists. He was born in Derby, the child of a successful silk-manufacturer. His father was a Baptist and his mother a Unitarian, so Thomas was not baptised until he requested it himself during his school days. In 1847, he entered St John's College, Cambridge.

Fr Bridgett was well known as both preacher and writer

Bridgett was not as exposed at Cambridge to the feverish religious disputes that wracked Oxford, but he was reading theology with a view to entering the ministry of the Church of England. Apart from some holidays abroad, his contacts with Catholicism were slight. As he departed for the long vacation at the end of the academic year of 1850, he remarked to a friend: "It is not likely that I shall return to Cambridge, but if I do, I shall be a thorough Protestant, and not a High Church Anglican." In May, he attended some of Newman's *Lectures on the difficulties of Anglicans* in London. By June, he was taking steps to be received into the Roman Catholic Church at the London Oratory. Bridgett was twenty-one years of age. As he had foreseen, he did not return to Cambridge. He was prevented from taking his degree without acknowledging the Anglican *Articles of Religion* and *Royal Supremacy*, which, as a Catholic, he was unable to do.

Soon after this, he made a retreat at the Redemptorist house in Hanley Castle. He had entered Cambridge intending to be ordained. The vocation to priesthood remained, but it could now only be fulfilled in the Catholic Church. He felt little attraction to Newman's Oratory as he believed its members were straining too hard to be ultra-Catholic and, "I wished to be thoroughly Catholic, but among those to whom it came easily and harmoniously." His reading of the life of St Alphonsus and a meeting with Louis de Buggenoms steered him towards the Redemptorists. In September 1850, after a mere three months as a Catholic, he was on his way to the novitiate in Belgium along with a young Irishman, William Plunkett, son of the Earl of Fingall.

Bridgett received the fullest Catholic theological education of all the converts of his generation. It included five years of ecclesiastical studies in Wittem, in Holland. He returned to England to become a member of the Clapham community in 1856. The years 1862 to 1871 were spent in Ireland as a missioner and retreat director, especially to clergy. He was an outstanding success as rector of Mount St Alphonsus in Limerick (1865–71), where he introduced the Archconfraternity of the Holy Family, founded a Catholic lending library and was responsible for the building of the chapel in honour of the Mother of Perpetual Help. He returned to Clapham as rector from 1871 to 1874. Further terms followed as rector in Limerick (1881 to 1884), and of the house of studies at Teignmouth (1893 to 1894).

When ill-health prevented him from going on missions and retreats, Bridgett dedicated his time to writing on subjects of theological and historical interest. When in Clapham, he spent many hours reading in the British Museum, but he was not ashamed to use helpers to cull a vast amount of literature. His writings display an encyclopaedic knowledge of English Catholic history, for example *Our Lady's Dowry: Devotion to the Blessed Virgin Mary in England* (1875), *The History of the Holy Eucharist in Great Britain* (1881), *The Life of Blessed John Fisher* (1888). His reputation as a writer introduced him to a growing circle of intellectual Catholics in Britain including Frederic Baron von Hügel, the lay apologist and theologian, who became a regular correspondent. Thomas Bridgett died in Clapham in 1899.

The Recusant

Edmund Vaughan was two years older than Thomas Bridgett, but a year junior to him in profession. He was a member of the Vaughan family of Courtfield who had continued to be loyal to the Catholic faith throughout the penal period. Edmund had been educated at Stonyhurst by the Jesuits. He taught for some time in Oscott College before applying to join the seminary. When he had reached deaconal orders, he applied to join the Redemptorists and, after his novitiate in Belgium, he was professed in 1852 along with Robert Coffin.

Vaughan then embarked on a lengthy ministry as a preacher of parish missions from the communities of Clapham and Bishop Eton. In 1867, he became superior of St Mary's, Kinnoull, near Perth, the first monastery to be opened in Scotland since the Reformation. He then ventured further afield. In 1882, with four priests and two Brothers, he left to establish the Redemptorists in Australia, where scattered settlements of Catholics, many of them poor Irish, made the parish mission apostolate attractive to the bishops. Edmund's brother, William, was bishop of Plymouth. The next generation of the family gave even more of its children to the service of the Church. One nephew, Roger, a Benedictine, became archbishop of Sydney, another, Herbert, cardinal archbishop of Westminster, Francis, bishop of Menevia, and a fourth, John, auxiliary bishop of Salford. This was in addition to two others who became priests, and five nieces who became nuns. Edmund was proposed as archbishop of Sydney in succession to his nephew, but his nomination was resisted by the clergy of the diocese who were Irish in the main and wanted one of their own.

Fr Vaughan returned to England and became provincial in 1894. He died at Bishop Eton, Liverpool, in 1908. Edmund Vaughan was a gifted hymn writer. Originally composed for use on parish missions, many of his hymns are still sung today, for example: *God of Mercy and Compassion*, *Look down O Mother Mary*, and *O Bread of Heaven*.

Fr Edmund Vaughan belonged to a distinguished old Catholic family, many of whose members gave service to the Church

The Redemptorists Today

Although the decline in numbers entering religious life has affected the Redemptorists as much as every other religious congregation in Britain, it nevertheless tries to be faithful to the tradition it has received.

The Redemptorists have always prided themselves in being "an order of preachers". Even in the ordinary ministry of their own churches, preaching has an important place. The parish mission apostolate continues to bring Redemptorists, along with lay co-workers, to parishes to preach a mission, retreat or novena for a week or more. Missions can be a time of renewal and celebration for a parish.

Although parish work was not encouraged by the early Redemptorist Rule, it has been a feature of the apostolic life of the London Province from the beginning. It currently runs parishes in London (Clapham), Birmingham (Erdington) and Liverpool (Bishop Eton). Alphonsus wanted the members of his congregation to be close to ordinary people and to share the joys and sorrows, the hopes and disappointments of daily life with them. That remains a central feature of parish ministry – from the joyful welcoming of new life in baptism, to the celebration of death in the hope of resurrection that is the mark of the Christian funeral. Redemptorists are involved in other pastoral projects, such as chaplains to hospitals and prisons. The Redemptorists run a renewal centre, where lay-folk, religious and clergy can recharge their spiritual and intellectual batteries, on the edge of the highlands at Kinnoull.

The first overseas mission to spring from the London Province was Australia. When the Province was divided, Australia became part of the Irish Province and eventually an independent Province in its own right. London was not left without a mission, since already in 1912, it had sent the first Redemptorists to South Africa. By 1989, it had done well enough, in terms of local vocations to the priesthood and Brotherhood, to become an independent Province. The region of Zimbabwe remains united to the mother Province. Today it has three communities and an increasing number of students.

For over fifty years, Redemptorists of the London Province have undertaken what Redemptorists call "the apostolate of the pen". A community at Chawton is dedicated to the production of various kinds of print media for the service of the Gospel and liturgy. They include books of reflection and popular theology, aids for the celebration of the sacraments and the different stages of life's journey. The members of the publications team are not exclusively Redemptorists: lay men and women also dedicate their skills to the ever diversifying work of publication.

A Place of Welcome

London's unique place in the world has made Clapham, since the beginning, a place to which Redemptorists throng. For some, it has been a stopping-off point on their missionary journeys between countries or continents. For others, it has been a place to pursue specialist education or training in theology, languages, administration or technical skills.

For many, notably for brethren from the European mainland, it has been a place of refuge in difficult times. Throughout the nineteenth and twentieth centuries, wars, revolutions and changes in the political climate forced many religious groups to leave their homelands. We have seen in this narrative how the first Redemptorists to come to England included men who were forced to leave Austria by revolution in the 1840s. During the 1870s, a series of laws and restrictions on religious orders in the newly unified Germany led to the *Kulturkampf* or the "cultural struggle". Some of the Redemptorists sought refuge in England. Two or three decades later, it was the turn of France. The laws declaring separation of Church and state in France in 1905 included a series of laws forbidding Religious to live together or to hold property. As a result, many were forced to flee. Many found refuge in Belgium and elsewhere but a sizeable number came to Britain.

To all of them, Clapham opened its doors and provided a place of welcome for at least a time. It may be a relatively quiet London parish, but Clapham is known around the Redemptorist world.

4. Architects and Artists

We owe the beauty of St Mary's to the imagination of the architects who, at different moments in its history, created a sacred space for the prayer and recollection of a growing worshipping community, and to the artists and craft-workers who adorned the building.

The majority of these are anonymous – the iron workers who made the screens, the stained-glass window makers, the carvers of wood and stone, the painters and the tile-layers. As in most Catholic churches, much of what we find in Clapham is repository art – the mass-produced statuary or holy pictures provided by big name producers. One of the best known providers of statues and stained glass for Catholic churches throughout the nineteenth and twentieth centuries was the German firm of *Mayer*, founded in 1847, and which was soon exporting its wares to Britain, Ireland and the United States where there was a surge in new church buildings. Some of the statues in St Mary's were provided by this firm. But there is also a good deal of original work that testifies to the growing self-confidence of the English Catholic community in its artistic heritage.

The First Architect: William Wilkinson Wardell

The architect who laid out the plans for St Mary's was William Wilkinson Wardell. Born in 1823 in Poplar, London, where his parents were in charge of the workhouse, Wardell embarked on a career as a civil engineer, but soon switched his interest to architecture under the influence of Augustus Welby Pugin (1812–1852). Pugin was a revolutionary force in British architecture in the Victorian age. In 1834 he converted to the Roman Catholic faith, which his French *émigré* father had abandoned. Two years later, he published a book called *Contrasts*, which was not only a call to return to the ideals of medieval art and architecture, but also to return to the faith and social structures that supported them. In many respects, Pugin's artistic revolution fed into the Oxford Movement which was calling for a reappraisal of the Catholic roots of the Anglican Church. It is scarcely surprising that Wardell became a Catholic at the age of twenty, and adopted as his motto the words, *Inveni quod quaesivi* ("I have found him whom I sought") from the biblical *Song of Songs*. His architectural practice was helped by his association with Pugin. On the strength of it, he was able to marry a few years later. It has been estimated that between 1846 and 1858 he designed, or was responsible for major refurbishment of, more than thirty churches in England.

William Wilkinson Wardell was the architect of St Mary's

Wardell was chosen as architect for the proposed Redemptorist church at Clapham by the superior, Fr Frederick de Held. His plans were for a church with a sanctuary, nave and two aisles. Only one thing in the original plan did not meet with de Held's approval. Pugin made the medieval "rood screen" a feature of the internal design of his churches. The rood screen was an elaborately carved wooden partition around the sanctuary, surmounted by a crucifix, often flanked by the figures of Mary and the Beloved Disciple. Although it had been a feature of medieval churches, and examples can still be seen in many English cathedrals, its original function had been essentially practical rather than decorative – to shield the clergy from cold breezes during the celebration of the long offices in choir. Counter-reformation changes in the style of building and decoration of Catholic churches meant the end of the rood screen, as it blocked the people's view of what was going on at the altar. As can be seen from St Mary's, de Held won and the view of the celebration of Mass at the altar was uninterrupted.

Ill-health forced Wardell to emigrate to Australia where he became the leading Catholic church architect and a major figure of his generation in Australian architecture. His most important churches are the cathedrals of Sydney and Melbourne. He was a genuinely devout man: in his homes, whether in England or Australia, a room was set aside as a chapel where he prayed several times daily. His rosary beads and prayer book, the traditional English *Garden of the Soul*, have been preserved and show signs of constant use. A prayer he composed addresses Our Lady as "my patroness, my mother, and my advocate with God … I consecrate myself for ever, with all that belongs to me, to thy service."

John Francis Bentley 1839–1902

John Francis Bentley is best known as the architect who designed Westminster Cathedral, the most prestigious Catholic building planned and built at the intersection of the nineteenth and twentieth centuries. Born in Doncaster in 1839, he belonged to a family of seventeen children. His religious background was Low Church and, according to his daughter and biographer, he retained all his life a certain Puritanism of life and habit (Winefride de l'Hôpital, *Westminster Cathedral and its Architect*, vol 2, 1919, 359). As a young man, he was apprenticed first to a builder who discerned that his talents lay more in the field of architecture. By the age of twenty, Bentley had worked on some church projects, including the extension of the Jesuit church in Farm Street, London. It was at this time that his religious search led him into the Catholic Church. It is said that recovery from serious illness which he ascribed to the Blessed Virgin shortened the journey, and he was baptised by Cardinal Wiseman in 1862. For the next ten years or so of his life, Bentley's work was in the line of relatively small religious commissions.

During this time, he made the acquaintance of the Redemptorists, particularly Frs Coffin and Vaughan, who remained friends all his life. Through this contact, he did his first work for the Redemptorist church of the Annunciation at Bishop Eton, Liverpool. The church on the site had been designed by Edward Pugin, but when the Redemptorists took over the house and planned an extension to the church, Bentley was appointed architect and, among other works, he designed a new high altar and a shrine for the icon of Our Lady of Perpetual Help, the first to be venerated in England.

Professional success made it possible for Bentley to move house into the comparatively affluent suburb of Clapham where he became a member of the parish, and, as his daughter wrote, "the passing of the years was to bring an ever growing intimacy with St Mary's and on which for as long as the building may endure, his seal is now indelibly impressed".

Bentley made three major contributions to the site. The first was the exquisite chapel in honour of Our Lady of Perpetual Help, the second the monastery building and finally the south transept with its accompanying modifications of Wardell's existing building. He also designed some of the stained glass. Details of the work will be considered in the appropriate contexts elsewhere in this guide.

John F. Bentley died in 1902 and was buried from St Mary's. The following year, his widow paid for the decorative grille around the sanctuary: her husband is commemorated in a bronze plaque let into the sanctuary steps. Bentley was succeeded as head of the firm by his son, Osmund, who also contributed to the work on St Mary's, notably the construction and decoration of the chapel in honour of St Gerard, which mirrors his father's Lady Chapel on the opposite aisle.

Bernard Cox

The next architect to make a major contribution to St Mary's, Clapham, was George Bernard Cox of Birmingham. Many of the churches he designed survive in the Midlands, including the Franciscan Friary, Olton, the Assumption, Maryvale, and the Sacred Heart and St Margaret Mary, Birmingham. The addition of Bentley's transept was not sufficient to cope with the growing congregations at St Mary's. There was little room for extension on the site. Two shops fronting on to Clapham Park Road were acquired in 1926 and Cox drew up plans for an extension which was completed and blessed in 1930.

Sir Ninian Comper

John Ninian Comper was a Scottish-born architect, and the last in a line of distinguished architects of the Gothic Revival. His contribution to St Mary's is limited to work done in the community chapel, which is not open to the public, at the time of the celebration of the centenary in 1948. Together with his son, John B. Sebastian Comper, he was consulted regarding the restoration of the chapel which was part of Bentley's transept. Comper was eighty-four years old when he undertook the work. He re-gilded Bentley's reredos and added to it images of four saints: St Joseph, and three Redemptorists: Alphonsus, Clement and Gerard. Sebastian Comper designed the frontal for the altar and a sunburst display of rays behind the large crucifix, and planned the stencilling of the walls. Wisely, they decided to leave Bentley's ceiling untouched. The chapel is a gem of the Gothic style. Sir Ninian Comper was knighted in 1950 and lived to the advanced age of ninety-six. His ashes were buried in Westminster Abbey.

The Community Chapel restored by Ninian Comper

Joseph Anton Settegast

Joseph Anton Settegast (1813–1890) was the German artist responsible for the fresco of the Last Judgment on the chancel arch. He was one of the last members of a movement of German-speaking Catholic artists called the "Nazarene School" (*Nazarener Schule*). The "Nazareners" were young artists in the early years of the nineteenth century who aspired to return to a form of art which embodied spiritual values and highlighted the importance of narrating a story through the use of colour, seeking their inspiration in artists of the late Middle Ages and early Renaissance, whose work was essentially religious. The "Nazareners" were, in many respects, the forerunners of a similar British movement known as the "Pre-Raphaelites". Settegast was living in Koblenz when he was given the commission to paint the arch. Koblenz at that time was the seat of the vicar general of the Redemptorists for the region north of the Alps, so it is likely that Settegast's work was familiar to Redemptorists like Fr de Held who probably chose him for the work in Clapham.

There are other interesting associations between the "Nazareners" and the Redemptorists. One of the founders of the movement, Johann Friedrich Overbeck, was a member of the circle of St Clement Hofbauer in Vienna, and Settegast's teacher, Philip Veit, was the son and stepson of two other members of the Hofbauer circle, Dorothea and Friedrich Schlegel. Veit had revived the art of fresco-painting among the "Nazareners" and probably initiated Settegast into the technique. It took the artist six months to complete the work, as he had to work directly on wet plaster.

From a series of letters between the artist and his wife (published in an article on the fresco in the *South London News*, 5 January, 1977), we know that the work took place between August and October 1854. The letters are often humorous in their comments. Settegast mentions, for example, that Cardinal Wiseman wanted to see the work in progress when he came to celebrate the feast of St Alphonsus, "but naturally being such a heavy man, he could not mount the scaffolding". He also observed that, while English churches attempted the great Masses of the German masters like Mozart and Haydn, they were not very good, lacking as they did the orchestral accompaniment of the originals, and had to rely on the organ alone: Mass for the feast of St Alphonsus was "particularly bad".

By the early twentieth century the fresco was deteriorating. It was restored by the Belgian firm of *Van Linthout* in 1926, who chose the expedient of re-painting the scene on canvas and then fixing this over the existing mural. Little is known about *Van Linthout*, but the firm is associated with the artwork in some of the Cox-designed churches mentioned above, and, since he was beginning his work at St Mary's at this time, it was probably he who chose them to restore the fresco.

Margaret Agnes Rope (Sr Margaret of the Mother of God ODC)

Only a few of the designers of the stained glass windows can be identified with any certainty. The two earliest, the great window over the high altar and the one near the organ, are in the style of the Gothic Revival, reminiscent of some of the surviving windows of the elder Pugin and which Wardell or someone from his workshop imitated. Bentley certainly designed the St Clement window in the south transept, the windows depicting the Old Testament "types" of Mary in the Lady Chapel and the "window of the angels" over the confessional next to it. Another artist whose work can be identified is Margaret Agnes Rope. Like many of those associated with St Mary's, Margaret Rope (1882–1953) was a convert from Anglicanism. After the early death of her husband, Margaret's mother converted to Catholicism, bringing five of her six children into the Church with her. Margaret studied art in Birmingham, specialising in stained glass and enamelling. She entered the Carmelite Convent at Woodbridge, Suffolk, where she was able to continue designing glass and so contributed to the community's income. For Clapham, she designed the Holy Family window at the rear of the church and a set of three lancets in what was then St Alphonsus's chapel in the tower: that space is now occupied by a small repository. The subjects are a Virgin and Child, the Crucifixion and the Blessed Sacrament.

5. Guide to the Church

Although generally known as St Mary's, the full title of the church is "Our Immaculate Lady of Victories". This was the title of the first Redemptorist foundation in England, at Falmouth in Cornwall, and it combines two traditional titles of Mary, namely, the Immaculate Conception and Our Lady of Victories.

Clapham has always kept the feast of the Holy Rosary, 7 October, as its patronal feast. A feast under the title of Our Lady of Victories was instituted in thanksgiving for the Christian victory over the Turks at the naval Battle of Lepanto in 1571. Two years later, the title was altered to Our Lady of the Rosary. Examples of churches dedicated to Our Lady of Victories include Sancta Maria delle Vittorie in Rome (where Bernini's famous statue of St Teresa of Avila is found), and Notre Dame des Victoires in Paris. It is probably the latter that has the closest link to Clapham. Both Fathers Lempfried and de Buggenoms, founders of the Falmouth mission, had celebrated Mass in it while visiting Paris.

External View

1. Front of the Church

St Mary's is constructed from Kentish ragstone, with softer and paler Caen stone as surrounds for archways and windows. The front is best observed from the opposite side of Clapham Park Road. The first striking feature is the tower and spire which soar to a combined height of 154 feet (47 metres). The tower is 69 feet (21 metres) high and the spire measures 85 feet (26 metres). The tower houses a peal of eight bells and this is the only Roman Catholic church in London with a complete peal.

On the front of the church there are two statues in niches. On the tower side is St Alphonsus Liguori, clothed as a bishop. The statue on the other side of the entrance door depicts St Gerard Majella as a young man, wearing the habit of the Order. By his side is a vase of lilies (symbol of chastity) and a skull (symbol of mortality). The main entrance to the church is no longer in use. The heavy oak door with black iron furniture is set within an archway. At the summit of the archway, is a small niche with an image of Christ in Majesty, while two smaller figures kneel beneath. That on the right, in bishop's mitre and carrying a crozier, is Alphonsus Liguori, the other wears the habit of the Redemptorist Order and may be intended to represent some of the members of the Order who had not yet been canonised.

Guide to the Church

Floor Plan of the Church

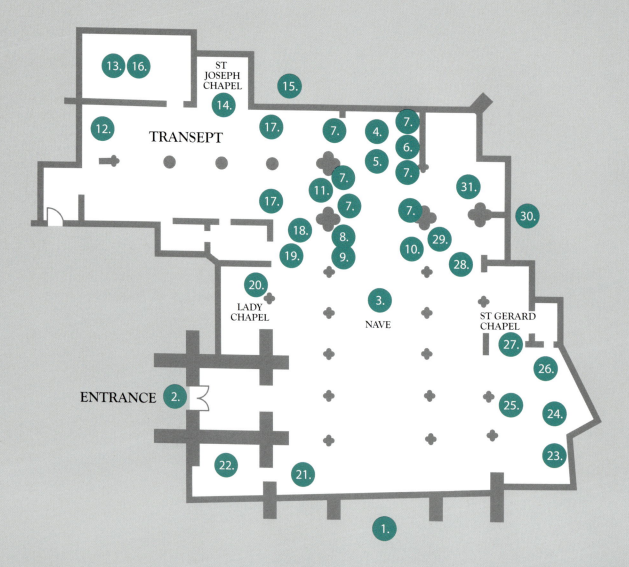

52

Church and Monastery seen from the garden

2. The Entrance

A gateway in Clapham Park Road leads to the entrance to the church and monastery. Opposite the entrance is the graceful War Memorial Cross, commemorating members of the Redemptorist Congregation and parishioners who had fallen in the First World War. It was designed by Sir Giles Gilbert Scott and dedicated in 1920.

Over the entrance door to the church is a carved medallion depicting the Annunciation, when Mary was told by the Archangel Gabriel that she was to be the mother of the Saviour. This is a favourite Marian scene and is depicted several times in the church. Under the main scene, two angels swing incense thuribles, a sign that this scene is viewed as a sacred mystery of faith. That on the right represents the coats of arms of the Redemptorist Congregation and the family arms of St Alphonsus Liguori. The porch is lit by two windows set up relatively high, each formed by two lancets. On the right side, stone tablets record the deceased of the Redemptorist community who had lived in the house since its foundation. The earliest is Brother Andrew Ward who died in 1861. The ceiling vaults spring from four carved heads on the corners of the porch, representing the symbols of the writers of the four Gospels. Beginning from the left of the door in the church, these are Matthew (symbol, a winged ox), Mark (winged lion), Luke (a human being – behind the entrance door) and John (an eagle). There is a small holy water font in a recessed niche at the right hand side of the door to allow worshippers to bless themselves.

On the ceiling, there is a delightful little medallion that will likely go unnoticed, of the Blessed Virgin Mary clothed in blue: it depicts her wearing a golden crown and surrounded by angels. It is probably intended to represent the assumption. It also represents a value of medieval art which was appreciated by those who pioneered the Gothic Revival, namely, that beauty was intended to give glory to God. Sometimes, an exquisitely beautiful piece of work is out of human sight, and seen only by the angels!

Guide to the Church

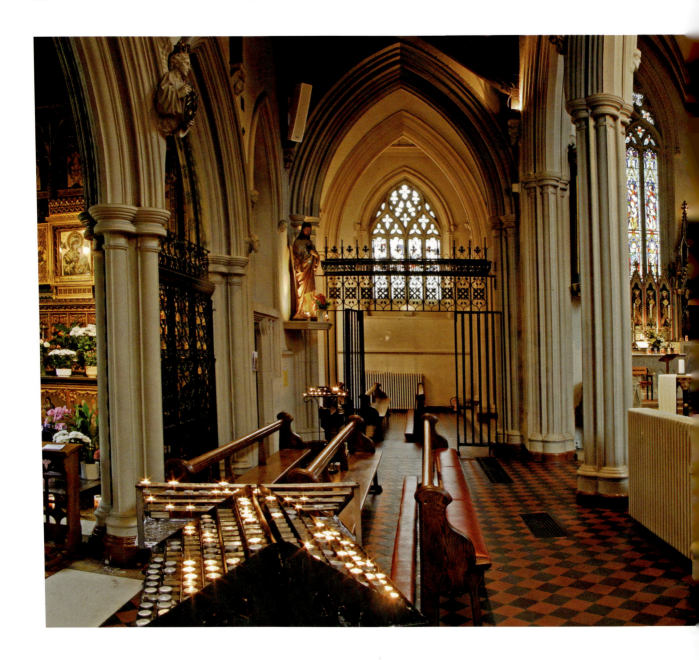

Guide to the Church

Panoramic view of St Mary's

Fresco detail: Christ in Majesty with the Blessed Virgin and John the Baptist

High Altar and Sanctuary

Interior – View of the Sanctuary from the Nave

We will begin our tour of the interior of the church by going to the end of the nave and looking towards the sanctuary.

3. The Fresco on the Chancel Arch

The fresco on the arch above the sanctuary or chancel, depicts the Last Judgement. It is the work of the German artist Josef Anton Settegast (1813–1890). He belonged to the artistic movement known as the *Nazarener School*, which flourished in the mid-nineteenth century and had some associations with the Redemptorist Congregation. The original fresco, which was painted directly on to plaster, had begun to show signs of disintegration so it was restored in 1926 by the Belgian firm of Van Linthout. They chose the expedient of repainting the scene on to canvas and then fixing it to the existing mural. The Final Judgement or "Doom" (hence "Doom's Day") was a common theme in medieval church art. It was often depicted on the east wall of the church, directly above the altar, or as in this case, on the chancel arch, so that the thought of their own judgement might be always before the minds of the congregation. The best known example of a Last Judgement, but from a slightly earlier period, is the great Michelangelo fresco in the Sistine Chapel in Rome.

Settegast has depicted Christ in Majesty, surrounded by a rainbow, an allusion to the account of the one seated on the throne in the Book of Revelation "who looks like jasper and carnelian, and around the throne is a rainbow that looks like an emerald" (Revelation 4:3). Mary, crowned but with her hands crossed modestly on her breast, occupies a seat to his right. This is another allusion to a biblical text frequently used in the liturgy of the Blessed Virgin Mary: "at your right stands the queen in gold of Ophir" (Psalm 45:9). On either side are the apostles in fulfilment of the promise Jesus had made to them: "Truly I tell you, at the renewal of all things, when the Son of Man is seated on the throne of his glory, you who have followed me will also sit on twelve thrones, judging the twelve tribes of Israel" (Matthew 19:28). There is a single standing figure who appears to stride confidently forward – John the Baptist, the messenger of the one who is to come. He holds a banner with the words (in Latin), "Behold the Lamb of God." Where the fresco moves into the narrower space of the archway, there are figures of angels, blowing trumpets to rouse the dead to attend the judgment: "He will send out his angels with a loud trumpet call, and they will gather his elect from the four winds, from one end of heaven to the other" (Matthew 24:31). The congregation, standing or kneeling in their places, would probably have found it relatively simple to imagine themselves as the people gathered for judgement.

4. The Great East Window

The sanctuary is composed of two bays and is dominated by the colourful stained-glass window in the same Gothic style as the rest of the church. The upper part is filled with coloured glass in abstract patterns. The colours, predominantly red and blue, the traditional colours of Christ and his mother, are remarkably vibrant, especially when the sun shines through the window. The main section of the window can be divided into three sections, each consisting of two lancet windows with two main parts (except for the central section). The lancets are again divided into two sections – a figure set within a

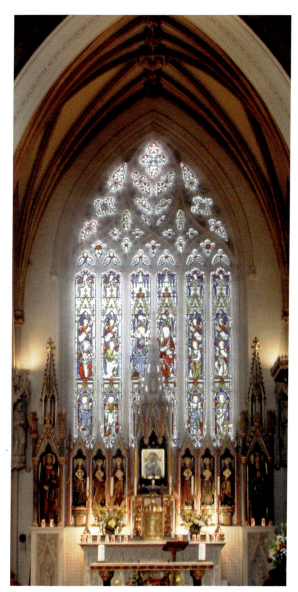

The Great East Window

Detail of Angels from East Window

stylised canopy and a lower register of figures. Although the central section is somewhat obscured by the central pinnacle of the altar reredos, its subject contains the theme of the whole window. On the right-hand panel, Christ, arrayed in royal red and wearing a crown, holds the orb in one hand, while his right is raised in blessing. On the left-hand panel, Mary arrayed in blue and crowned with gold, inclines towards her Son. The Catholic congregation would have recognised this as the "fifth glorious mystery" of the Rosary, the crowning of Mary as Queen of Heaven. The main subjects on each side are the archangels, each identified by a symbol. Beginning on the far left and reading across, the angels are Michael ("Who is like God?"), with sword and shield representing the defender of Israel and the Church, Raphael ("God heals"), known from the Book of Tobit and who holds the fish, whose gall was used to cure the blindness of Tobias. Nearest to Christ is Gabriel ("God is my strength"), messenger of the annunciation, carrying the lily which is a Marian symbol of purity. The final angel, Uriel, does not often figure on Catholic lists of archangels. He is named in the apocryphal biblical book, 4 Esdras 4:1. The name Uriel means "God is my light", so his symbol is the sun.

The lower register contains images of virgin martyrs, each carrying her symbol, either representing her name or the way in which she met her death. Beginning on the left – Agnes with a lamb (Latin, *agnus*), Catherine with the wheel and sword, Cecilia, patroness of musicians, with the harp, Lucy with the dish holding her eyes, as she was blinded during her martyrdom, Barbara, with the tower in which her father locked her as a protection on account of her beauty, and Agatha with pincers, used in tearing her body during her martyrdom.

5. The High Altar

The high altar with the tabernacle would have been the original focus of the church. It is in a Gothic style. The central section, crowned with a pinnacle, marks the location of the tabernacle. The space, now occupied by an image of the Blessed Virgin, would originally have contained a crucifix and on certain occasions it was used for showing the Blessed Sacrament enclosed in a monstrance for eucharistic adoration. It is balanced by two smaller pinnacles on each side. The pinnacle on the left shows Christ the King and that on the right, Mary as Queen of Heaven. On each side, three angels bear medallions carrying symbols of the passion – (from left) the crown of thorns, the cross, ladder and lance, the seamless garment for which the soldiers cast lots, the pillar and scourge, the nails with the hammer and pliers, and the five wounds. Below the figures of Christ and his mother, the two lowest panels tell the story of the annunciation – on the left, the angel Gabriel and on the right Mary, with her symbol of the lily. The figures on the reredos are coloured. Judging from some of the older photographs that have survived, the figures may originally have been of a relatively neutral shade, but the additional colour and gilding give a more dramatic appearance to the sanctuary.

The front of the altar has seven panels. The smaller, outer panels reflect the motif of the angels with the medallions of the passion. The five larger ones depict the five sorrowful mysteries of the rosary, except that the fifth, the crucifixion, has been given pride of place at the centre. Beginning from the left, they represent the prayer of Jesus in the garden of Gethsemane (Mark 14:32–42), the scourging at the pillar (John 19:1), the crowning with thorns (John 19:2) and Jesus carrying his cross to Calvary (John 19:17).

The Tabernacle [centre of the High Altar]

Tabernacle on the High Altar

When the church was built, the dominant eucharistic theology of the day, and one certainly shared by the Redemptorists, was that the Eucharist continued to make present the sacrifice of Calvary and that the consecrated host remained a living memorial of the Lord's passion and of his abiding presence. A more contemporary theology of the Eucharist will also lay stress on it as the banquet of eternal life to be shared in memory of the Crucified and Risen Lord. The root of this theology is in the scriptures. This first part of that traditional theology, with its emphasis on the passion of Christ, is clearly reflected in the decoration of the high altar.

The second aspect is represented by the tabernacle. The domed tabernacle on the altar today was the gift of Miss K. Mahony of the parish in memory of her parents. It is one of Bentley's late works and was completed shortly before his death in 1902. It is made from beaten copper with decorations of lapis lazuli and mother of pearl. Around the dome of the tabernacle, a Latin inscription reads: *Cor Jesu sacratissimum miserere nobis* ("Most Sacred Heart of Jesus, have mercy on us"). There is also a symbol of the Sacred Heart of Jesus on the door. On the top of the tabernacle, is a figure of "the pelican in her piety". This was an image used in medieval art and heraldry that depicted a mother pelican piercing her breast to make her heart's blood flow as nourishment for her young. It was often used as an image of Christ's love in the Eucharist, giving himself as food to the believer. St Thomas Aquinas in his eucharistic hymn, *Adoro Te*, writes: "Lord Jesus, good pelican, wash me clean with your blood, one drop of which can free the entire world of all its sins."

6. Sedilia and Piscina

On the wall at the right of the altar, under four ornate canopies, are seats (*sedilia*) for the priests celebrating High Mass, along with a fourth niche; closest to the altar another that was intended as a basin (*piscina*). The pre-Vatican II rite for the celebration of Mass had two basic forms – "Low Mass" celebrated in a low tone of voice by one priest with the assistance of at least one server, and "High (or Solemn) Mass" which was sung with the assistance of a choir, many servers and a deacon and subdeacon. At certain points in the service, the priests sat on the *sedilia*. A small carving on the back of each seat gives the rank of the minister for whom it was intended. Nearest the nave, water and wine cruets indicated this as a seat for the subdeacon, who brought the cruets of wine and water at the preparation of the gifts during the liturgy. The central niche is for the celebrant, symbolised by the chalice and host. The third was for the deacon, whose symbol is the book of the Gospels, which he proclaimed at Mass.

The ornamentation of the fourth niche, the *piscina*, is somewhat subdued. The Latin word means "little fishpond". In church architecture, it is applied to a shallow basin which, during the Middle Ages, was used for washing the vessels used at Mass, so that the water could drain into a clean place. Although the Tridentine Rite did not permit a *piscina* to be used for this purpose, the architects of the Gothic revival invariably placed one in the sanctuary of their churches but usually with a shelf, as here, so that it could serve as a small table for the wine and water needed for the celebration of Mass.

7. Saints

Each of the six pillars has a saint. The two central ones facing each other are, on the left, St Teresa of Avila and the prophet Isaiah. The remaining four on the corners represent the four evangelists. Teresa of Avila, the Spanish mystic, was one of the patrons of the Redemptorist Congregation. From its frequent citation in the New Testament, Isaiah is often called the "Fifth Gospel". In this representation he holds a book and a saw, reflecting a common tradition that he suffered martyrdom by being sawn in two.

8. Statue of the Blessed Virgin

The Statue of Our Lady was a gift from the mother of Fr Douglas

The original pulpit has been adopted as a liturgical ambo

At the entrance to the sanctuary, there is a statue of the Blessed Virgin Mary. It was a gift from Mrs Douglas, mother of Fr Douglas. Douglas was an only child, and his unexpected conversion to Roman Catholicism caused a rift with his mother, who sent a clergyman friend to Rome to try to talk him out of his decision. His ordination and entry to the Redemptorists added a further strain to this tense relationship. Mrs Douglas never entered the Catholic Church, but her gift of the statue is a lovely gesture of reconciliation. The little shrine in which it stands was raised higher up the pillar to enable the baptismal font to be placed at the entrance to the sanctuary.

9. Baptismal Font

This is the baptismal font originally designed for the church by Wardell. It has stood in various places in the course of its history. Bentley was invited to design a new font but he refused on the grounds that all his children had been baptised in the old one. The present location of the font enables the baptismal liturgy to be celebrated in the view of the congregation, heightening its place as a sacrament celebrated by the whole parish community.

10. Pulpit /Ambo

The pulpit originally had four panels bearing the symbols of the four evangelists. Over it is a soundboard which, in the days before amplification, enabled the preacher's voice to resound better. An image of a dove, symbol of the Holy Spirit, hovers over the one who preaches. In the refurbisment of the church, the pulpit was preserved but transformed into the *ambo*, the place from which the readings from scripture are proclaimed in the course of the liturgy. This required some redesign. The pulpit now has two sets of steps – one from the sanctuary for the celebrant and the other from the nave for the reader. To facilitate the second flight of steps, one of the panels was removed and with it the symbol of one of the evangelists.

The Sanctuary Grille commemorates the architect, John Francis Bentley

11. The Sanctuary Grille

The black iron grille between the sanctuary and the transept was erected in the early twentieth century. The step on the transept side has two brass memorial plates. The first says: "Pray for the soul of John and Mary Dell in whose memory this screen has been erected by their children." The second commemorates John Francis Bentley, the architect of additions to the church in the late nineteenth century and designer of the Lady Chapel: "Of your charity pray for the soul of John Francis Bentley who died ii (2nd) day of March in the year of Our Lord MCMII (1902) in whose memory this grille is erected by his wife."

The grille itself bears two inscriptions in gilt lettering. Closest to the altar: *Ego exaltatus a terra omnia traham ad me ipsum* ("And when I am lifted up from the earth, I will draw all things to myself", John 12:32). The other reads: *O res mirabilis manducat dominum pauper servus et humilis* ("Oh, something wonderous ! The body of God will nourish the poor, the slave, and the lowly"). The words are taken from the office hymn of *Corpus Christi*, which is better known from its shortened form as *Panis Angelicus*.

The Marriage of Joseph and Mary

The South Transept
The south transept of the church was completed in 1894 to cope with the increasing numbers of the parish. The architect, John F. Bentley, scrupulously respected the existing style of Wardell's original church. The transept has a row of pillars in the middle that forms two arcades over the single seating area. Entry to the transept is possible through an additional entrance near the monastery, with a small porch.

12. The Baptistery
Bentley had designed a small baptistery at the rear of the transept which was closed by a simple iron screen. It housed Wardell's original baptismal font. Baptismal fonts were commonly placed near the entrance to a church to emphasise the place of the sacrament as a moment of entry into the church. The liturgical reform of Vatican II, while continuing to regard it as a rite of initiation, emphasised the role of the community. The reordering of the church subsequent to the Council, placed the font closer to the sanctuary to facilitate the communal celebration of the sacrament. The original font is now situated in the sanctuary.

13. The Sacristy
An oak door under an archway leads to the sacristy. The archway over the door springs from two delicately carved heads of children. While it is impossible to identify them or any of the other carved heads at the base of the arches, it is tempting to surmise that they may have been based on the children of the architect who were baptised in this church.

14. The Chapel of St Joseph
A chapel of St Joseph, which originally stood in the south aisle, was relocated to its present position when the transept was added. The chapel is enclosed by a small altar rail. The original altar was restored by Bentley. The reredos contains a coloured statue of St Joseph and it is flanked by two scenes carved in relief.

Guide to the Church

Nativity – Detail from the reredos in St Joseph's Chapel

Death of St Joseph: Central Panel on the altar

The panel on the left depicts the marriage of Mary and Joseph. This scene is not described in the New Testament, but it appears in several apocryphal Gospels, notably the *Protoevanglium of James*, a popular text possibly written as early as the mid-second century. According to its narrative, Mary had been presented in the Temple at the age of three. When the time came for her to be married, the priests summoned the men of Israel who wished to marry her. Their staffs were taken and laid on the altar in the hope that God might indicate who was to marry her. When the high priest went to examine them later, the wood of Joseph's staff was found to have blossomed. A staff sprouting lilies (symbol of chastity) is now usually associated with St Joseph. The high priest conducts the marriage celebration against a background of fruiting vines. Just in front of Joseph, a rival breaks his staff over his knee, while behind him, another snaps his in frustration with his hands.

The panel on the right depicts a nativity scene. Above the stable, two groups of angels represent the heavenly choir praising God (Luke 2:13). Four of the angels carry musical instruments – the other two are presumably the singers. The instruments are (from left): harp, portative organ, pipe and lute. Below them is a thatched stable in which Mary and Joseph have laid the child in the manger. Joseph looks outside to see the shepherds arriving in two groups, on either side.

On the base of the altar, the main panel depicts the death of Joseph, with Jesus and Mary with him. Catholic tradition invokes Joseph as the patron of a happy death. The scene is witnessed by two angels who may also have come to bear his soul into paradise (Luke 16:22). At each side of the central scene, in two side panels, two angels carry scrolls that say *Pretiosa in conspectu Domini mors sanctorum eius* (Psalm 116:15) – "precious in the eyes of the Lord is the death of his saints."

Over the altar are two groups of stained-glass windows. The first set depicts the birth of Jesus in Bethlehem and the flight into Egypt. The second set depicts the finding of Jesus in the Temple by Mary and Joseph, and the family of Nazareth as an example for family industry and harmony. The windows bear the names of the donors or of those in whose

65

memory they were given – Laurence O'Mahony (died 1890), and his sister Anna (1893), and Osmond and Mary Josephine Lambert, a husband and wife who died within a few months of each other.

The fine coloured ceiling is supported by six crowned angels carrying scrolls that spell out the message *Vir fidelis multum laudabitur qui custos Domini judicabitur* ("The faithful man is greatly to be praised who was found fit to be the guardian of the Lord"). The words are based on Proverbs 28:20 and used as an antiphon in the old Latin office of St Joseph.

15. The Window in honour of St Clement

This window was designed by Bentley, but his daughter does not regard it as one of his most successful windows. The cartoons for it are in the monastery archives. Clement Hofbauer, a man from a farming background in Bohemia (present-day Czech Republic), by a variety of circumstances became the second founder of the Redemptorists. He is also one of the patrons of the city of Vienna. The window has four scenes. Working left to right, they depict: Clement's profession as a Redemptorist; Clement celebrating Mass; Clement the confessor, and Clement the preacher. The window is dedicated "In honour of Blessed Clement, Patron and Model of Redemptorists, to the memory of the fathers who have laboured in this church". It was erected by a subscription of the congregation attending St Mary's church to celebrate the beatification (last stage on the road to canonisation) of Clement in 1888, and it was dedicated on the feast of St Alphonsus 1896.

16. The Community Chapel

High on the wall are two windows. They were designed by Wardell, and were originally in the wall of the sanctuary that was removed to build the transept. Behind them is the community chapel where the Redemptorist community celebrates the daily office and other prayers. It, with the small gallery at the end of the transept for the use of the community, is only accessible from the monastery.

The community chapel was originally designed by Bentley as part of his transept but it is part of the monastery building. It was refurbished in 1948 in celebration of the Clapham centenary. The work was carried out under the direction of Sir Ninian Comper, and his son, Sebastian. Comper re-ordered Bentley's reredos, imposing on it three Redemptorist saints (Alphonsus, Clement and Gerard), with St Joseph occupying the fourth space. The brass tabernacle door has an image of the pelican. Bentley's ceiling was left unchanged, with its barrel vaulting and bands of darker and lighter green, on which the monogram of Jesus (IHS) and Mary (a Gothic

M) alternate in gold. The wall at the altar end and the doors were also painted in red, black and gold with stencilled symbols. The adjoining sacristy contains an enthroned Madonna with saints – Francis, Edward, Clare and Joseph. It is the work of Alexander Maximilian Seitz (1811–1888), a member of the *Nazarener School*, and was painted for Fr Edward Douglas, who gave it to Clapham.

17. The Statues of Ss John Fisher and Thomas More

On the side walls of the transept, are two small statues set on brackets. They represent John Fisher, bishop of Rochester (1469–1555), and Thomas More (1478–1555), chancellor of England. Both were executed under Henry VIII for opposing his divorce from Catherine of Aragon. They were beatified along with other English martyrs in 1886. More and Fisher were canonised in 1935. Their feast day is 22 June. A member of St Mary's community, Fr Thomas Bridgett, wrote early studies of both of them at the time of their beatification.

The South Aisle

This aisle can be closed off from the rest of the church as a security measure by locking the iron grille. The grille bears the inscription *Copiosa apud eum Redemptio* ("With him there is plentiful redemption" Psalm 130:7), the official motto of the Redemptorist Congregation.

18. The Way of the Cross

The Way of the Cross is a traditional devotion involving fourteen stations, or pauses for prayer, as one walks around the church, meditating on the passion and death of Jesus. St Alphonsus Liguori, founder of the Redemptorists, did much to popularise the devotion, and the prayers he composed for it are still commonly used. The stations that had been in Clapham since its foundation were, by the 1960s, beginning to show the need for restoration but they proved to be beyond repair. The present set was offered to the church through the apostolic delegate or papal ambassador. They had been made for ex-King Umberto of Italy by a wood carver from Bologna, called Giovanni Pella.

19. The Angel Window

Above the confessional whose entrance is recessed into the wall, there is a very pretty window depicting three angels. The two outer angels carry blue shields with the words, *Ave Maria* ("Hail Mary"). The middle angel's shield has a lily, a symbol of Mary's purity. The inscription at the bottom reads *Sub pennis eius sperabis* ("In his wings you will trust", Psalm 91:4). The window was designed by Bentley and given to the church as a gift.

The Stations of the Cross were a gift of ex-King Umberto of Italy

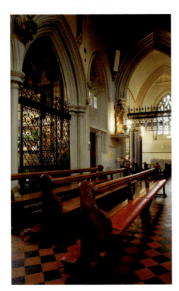

Lady Chapel Grille

20. The Lady Chapel

The Lady Chapel is the jewel of St Mary's and is regarded as one of the masterworks of John Francis Bentley. It is also a veritable theology of Mary in paint, stone, wood and metal. The architect has used traditional material and images, but several features, particularly the selection from the vast repertoire of liturgical texts and hymns in honour of the Virgin Mary, are a witness to the personal nature of his own faith.

Although the dedication of the church to St Mary made a separate Lady Chapel unnecessary, the gift of a Byzantine-style icon to the Redemptorist church in Rome by Pope Pius IX in 1866 put this image firmly at the heart of the devotional life of the Congregation. Although venerated in Rome, the icon was probably painted on the island of Crete in the late fifteenth century, and belongs to an icon type known as "The Theotokos (Mother of God) of the Passion". The earliest example of this type appeared as a fresco in a church in Cyprus and dates from about 1192. According to a legend associated with the Roman copy, it was stolen from a church on the island of Crete by an Italian merchant. In remorse for his theft, the icon was given to the small church of San Matteo, between the Roman basilicas of St Mary Major and St John Lateran. Here it acquired the title of *Madonna de Perpetuo Succurso* (Mother of Perpetual Help). In the middle of the seventeenth century, San Matteo came into the possession of the Irish Augustinian friars, who had been forced to leave their homeland by anti-Catholic laws. They remained in possession of it until the army of Napoleon arrived in Rome in 1798. Both the monastery and church were demolished in 1810. The friars had gone to live in another part of Rome, at the church of Santa Maria in Posterula. They had brought the icon with them, but as there was already a popular Marian image there, the one they brought was relegated to an inner chapel of the monastery.

A mention in the course of a sermon that its whereabouts were currently unknown jogged the memory of a young Redemptorist priest. As a boy, he had served Mass in Santa Maria in Posterula, where an elderly brother had told him the story of the icon. The icon was indeed where he had said it was, but it was in very poor condition and scarcely recognisable. The Redemptorists petitioned Pope Pius IX to have it transferred to their church on the Via Merulana, close to where San Matteo had once stood. After restoration, it was solemnly installed in the Redemptorist church of San Alfonso, whose construction costs, incidentally, had been borne by Fr Douglas, who had also defrayed the cost of St Mary's. Copies were sent to every Redemptorist community. Clapham's copy was solemnly exposed for public veneration on 11 December 1867. It was placed at the old St Joseph's altar at the head of the south aisle until a special place could be found for it. In 1883, John

Francis Bentley was asked to design a Lady Chapel off the south aisle of the church and it was completed the following year. It was built at the expense of Mrs Jane Louis, in memory of her husband, William John Louis, who had a particular devotion to the icon, and whose personal copy is now enshrined on the altar of the chapel.

Two arches open from the aisle into the chapel. The one nearest the sanctuary has an iron grille, designed by the architect. Picked out in gilt letters on the aisle side is the Latin inscription: *Sancta Maria, succurre miseris, iuva pusillanimes, refove flebiles* ("Holy Mary, succour the miserable, help the faint-hearted, cheer those that weep"). Taken from a sermon by Fulbert, bishop of Chartres (951–1029), the words were adopted as an antiphon for offices of the Blessed Virgin, including, with a small addition at the end, the office of Our Lady of Perpetual Help. On the inner side of the grille, the inscription reads, *Salve regina, mater misericordiae, vita, dulcedo et spes nostra salve* ("Hail, holy Queen, mother of mercy, hail our life, our sweetness and our hope"): these words would have been especially familiar, as this, both in Latin and in English, is one of the most familiar Marian prayers.

The Altar of Our Lady is always well supplied with flowers

On entering the chapel, one is struck by the deep blue colour of the walls. Bentley's daughter, probably drawing on his notes, has stressed how this deep colour is symbolic of the deep waters of pain through which Mary learned to understand and sympathise with human suffering, and which is the key to the title of "Perpetual Help". The somewhat sombre tone is relieved by the use of gold in the alternating symbols of the gothic "M" with a crown (initial of Mary) and the pomegranate, a symbol of new life and resurrection, associated with Mary. Just as Eve is associated with the fruit that led to the Fall, so Mary is associated with Christ who brings the fruit of new life.

What holds our attention, however, is the gleaming golden colour of the reredos that almost reaches the ceiling at the end of the chapel. It is over fifteen feet high and may be divided into four major sections.

Beginning at the top, a shallow canopy, supported on a fan vaulting, covers the whole. The vaulting forms three niches, each containing the figure of an angel. The angel in the centre holds a jar with a lily, traditional symbol of the Blessed Virgin Mary's purity. The angel in the left hand niche carries a scroll, the text of which reads *Tu honorificentia populi nostri* ("You are the honour of our people"). The scroll of the angel on the right reads *Tu advocato peccatorum* ("You are the advocate of sinners"). Both texts are taken from a medieval Marian hymn, *Tota Pulchra es Maria* ("You are all fair, Mary"). This hymn is essentially a chain or catena of biblical verses applied to Mary. The title, for example, is taken from the Song of Songs, in which the Lover says to the Bride "You are altogether beautiful, my love; there is no flaw in you" (Song of Songs 4:7). The first text is taken from the conclusion of the Book of Judith, in which Judith, who has just saved Israel by killing Holofernes, the Assyrian general, is praised as a heroine: the liturgy applies it to Mary as the personification of the New Jerusalem. Across the bottom of this section, there runs a band with yet another text: *Sancta Maria, succure cadenti, surgere qui curat populo* ("Holy

Mother, help the fallen, lift up the people, you who cure"). These words are taken from another Marian liturgical text, the *Alma Redemptoris Mater*, an antiphon especially associated with the seasons of Advent and Christmas.

In the central section, pride of place is given to the icon. In contrast to the predominant golden colour of the rest of the reredos, the background of this section is a deep Persian blue with patterns incised in a lighter blue and gold that give the impression of tapestry. The picture is set within a three-part frame (triptych). In the triptych, the large central panel holds the icon, while the two side panels, usually of the same length, but only half the width, can be closed as doors to conceal the icon. When open, the inner surface of these side panels reveals two angels swinging thuribles in the direction of the icon, a sign of veneration and respect. When the panels are closed, the image they form on the outside is the annunciation to Mary. Triptychs were closed either to protect the image or to mark penitential seasons when it was not deemed appropriate to display rich and beautiful things, for example the veiling of images during Passiontide. The older title of this icon-type was *Our Lady of the Passion*. A traditional story associated with it tells how the Christ Child had a dream of his Passion and ran in fear to his mother for comfort. He clings to Mary's hand, while looking over his shoulder towards one of the angels carrying the instruments of the Passion. Mary's gaze is turned, not towards her child, but to the one who prays before the icon. The gaze of Mary, both sorrowful and maternal, is an illustration of the familiar words of the *Salve Regina*: "turn then, most gracious advocate, thine eyes of mercy towards us." The sandal falling from the foot of the child may be a homely symbol of a child losing his footwear in his terrified flight from a frightening vision, but in the Bible, taking off a shoe or a sandal was a sign of laying aside a claim to property (Ruth 4:7-8). It recalls Paul's hymn to Christ who "emptied himself, taking the form of a slave" (Philippians 2:7–11). On the frame, immediately under the icon, is inscribed its Latin title, *Mater de Perpetuo Succurso*.

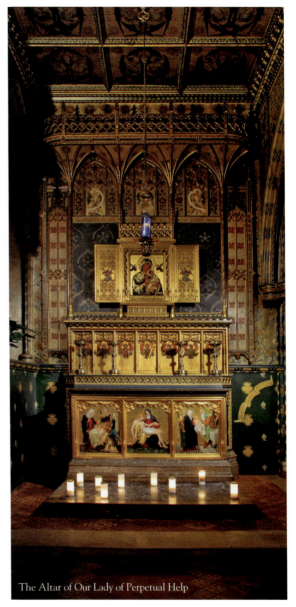

The Altar of Our Lady of Perpetual Help

Closed Triptych with Annunciation Scene

Eve from the stained glass in the Lady Chapel

Immediately under the picture, seven angels, each in its own frame, carry one of the instruments of the Passion, the central one carrying the cross. The same motif has already been noted in the high altar of the church. It is repeated here to highlight the motif of the Passion, which would have been prominent in Redemptorist spirituality and preaching at this time.

The altar would have been regarded as the most important element in the chapel. Mass would have been celebrated in it most days, since Clapham was the home of a religious community of priests, who would each have celebrated a private Mass (concelebration, or several priests celebrating at the same altar, was only introduced in the liturgical reforms of the 1960s) and all the altars in the church would have been required. The table of the altar (*mensa*) is Derbyshire marble: stone was required by the liturgical law of the time. It has a slate frontal, designed originally to be removed on occasions when the triptych was closed. The predominant colour of the frontal picks up the golden colour of the reredos. It contains three scenes whose mode of depiction and the costuming of the main characters recalls the style of medieval Flemish art. The first depicts the birth of Christ. Mary and Joseph stand near the manger, hands raised in ecstasy, while an angel in a blue dalmatic, the vestment of a deacon, kneels in adoration. The central image is a *pieta*, or to give it its medieval English name, *Our Lady of Pity*. Mary holds the bleeding body of her Son, while on the ground are instruments of the Passion – the crown of thorns and the nails. The central place given to this image seems to see it as the fulfilment of the scene prophesied by the icon, when Mary held the child in the comfort of her arms as he looked with terror on the cross and crown of thorns, which still lay in the future. The third scene depicts the presentation in the temple, when Simeon took the child in his arms and predicted that a sword would pierce the heart of Mary (Luke 2:35). The old woman, the prophetess Anna, looks on from the side.

The chapel is lit by three decorated windows, each consisting of three panels. The glass is tinted in such a way that it admits a silvery-golden light into the chapel. The subjects of all nine window panels are women of the Old Testament, many of whom Catholic tradition has identified as prototypes of Mary. In order (from left), they are: Eve (mother of the living, just as Mary is mother of the redeemed); Sarah (mother of the people of Israel, just as Mary is mother of the new Israel); Rebecca (the first mother of Israel after Sarah); Rachel (who endured years of barrenness before giving birth); Deborah (judge and prophet); Ruth (ancestor of David and named in St Matthew's genealogy of Jesus); Abigail (wife of David); Esther (who saved Israel by her prayers), and Judith (who risked her life to slay Holofernes, the enemy of Israel). An inscription records that the windows are dedicated to the memory of Anne Camilla MacDonald who departed this life on 29 July, in the year 1884.

Guide to the Church

Ceiling decoration: Lady Chapel

Invocation from Litany of Loreto: Queen of the Most Holy Rosary

The decoration of the ceiling is detailed and systematic. Three beams divide the ceiling and each section is further divided into two rows of three panels, making eighteen in all. The panels immediately above the altar area depict the six seraphim, each with six wings (Isaiah 6:2–7), wearing stoles crossed in front and highlighting the sacredness of the altar area. In the remaining twelve panels, the predominant symbols are roses with other plants and leaves, set against a light-coloured background, and each panel contains one of the titles of Mary from the *Litany of Loreto*. This Litany in honour of the Blessed Virgin emerged at the Italian Marian shrine of Loreto sometime in the late Middle Ages. From there it spread throughout Europe and became a popular devotion to Mary. It invokes Mary by a list of titles to invite the faithful to pray (the standard response is "Pray for us"). The titles are arranged in a number of sets: Mary as mother (twelve invocations), Mary as virgin (six invocations), biblical symbols of Mary (thirteen, for example, Tower of David, from the Song of Songs), Mary as helper of the faithful (four titles, for example, Health of the sick) and Mary as queen (thirteen titles, for example, Queen of angels).

The Litany of Loreto provides further inspiration for the decoration of the walls of the chapel, particularly in the upper arcades formed by the arches. The colour here is lighter, relieving the sombre blue that predominates in the lower part of the walls.

The Lady Chapel was intended to provide a place for personal prayer and meditation. It is seldom without flowers and candles left by devotees of Mary. The predominant note to which Bentley returns is that Mary is mother and advocate. The use of verses from familiar hymns, such as the *Salve Regina*, in the decoration underlines that teaching. The *Salve* had a special place in the spirituality of Redemptorists. Their founder devoted more than half of his classic book of Mariology, *The Glories of Mary*, to a commentary on it. Most of the day's religious observances concluded with its recitation, just as the profession of vows ended with a solemn singing of it. Bentley has chosen relatively few incidents from the life of Mary for illustration but what is striking in his chapel is the way in which the dominant note of redemption and Mary's part in it as mother and intercessor is stated through the symbols of the Passion and the icon of Perpetual Help.

21. The Window of the Holy Family

Continuing to the end of this aisle, we will see a fine stained-glass window in honour of the Holy Family. The Redemptorists cultivated devotion to the Holy Family, especially through the Confraternity of the Holy Family, founded in Belgium in 1844 by a layman called Henri Belletable, an army engineer, to promote strong family values among the emerging working classes, and confided to the pastoral care of the Redemptorists. Fr Thomas Bridgett, a member of the Clapham community, during an earlier period as rector in Limerick, founded in 1868 a branch of the confraternity which went on to become the largest confraternity in the world. The Clapham branch of the confraternity drew the bulk of its membership from women and it flourished until the middle of the twentieth century.

The window is the work of Margaret Agnes Rope (1882-1953), a stained-glass artist who continued to design and create glass even after she had entered a contemplative Carmelite monastery under the name of Sr Margaret of the Mother of God. It is composed of three lancets, each with two subjects and two inscriptions. In the central pane, Jesus the child stands with his hands outstretched. In the side panels, the corresponding images are of Mary and St Joseph. The inscription at the top reads, *Ubi caritas, Deus ibi est* ("Where there is love, God is there", the opening words of the chant for the *Mandatum* or liturgy of the washing of the feet on Maundy Thursday). In the lower half of each window, there are small representations of scenes in which all three members of the Holy Family appear together – the presentation of Jesus in the Temple (Luke 2:22–39), the Family at Nazareth and the finding of Jesus in the Temple (Luke 2: 41–51). The inscription at the bottom of the window reads *Illumina nos Domine exemplis familiae tuae et dirige pedes nostros in viam pacis* ("Enlighten us, O Lord, by the example of your family and guide our feet in the way of peace").

22. The Chapel of St Alphonsus

This chapel is usually locked, as it now serves as a small repository or religious goods shop. The door bears a very fine wood carving of Mary Magdalene. Originally intended for a confessional, it was the gift of Bernard Cox, architect of the 1930 extension to the church.

The centrepiece of the chapel is the reredos depicting the life of St Alphonsus. It was designed for the original altar of St Alphonsus (where the organ is today). The altar table was removed to the sanctuary, where it now serves as the altar "facing the people" for the daily Eucharist. Alphonsus's life is depicted in three scenes that cover representative moments of that life. In the first, as a young lawyer who has reached a moment of crisis in his profession, Alphonsus was forced to decide whether to return to the courts or to begin studies for the priesthood. As a sign of the latter, he chose to lay his nobleman's dress-sword at the feet of the statue of Our Lady of Ransom in a church near his home. The central section depicts Alphonsus the preacher. He was once preaching in a church in Foggia where there was a venerated picture of the Madonna. He experienced a time of ecstasy during his sermon. The third scene commemorates an unusual incident in the life of Alphonsus. On 21 September 1774, he fell unconscious after celebrating Mass, and remained in that state until the following morning, when he roused himself and asked to celebrate Mass for the repose of the soul of the pope at whose death he had assisted in spirit. It was several days before the news of the pope's death reached the remote part of Southern Italy where Alphonsus lived.

The three stained-glass windows (two on side walls and one over the altar) are also the work of Margaret Rope. They commemorate three devotions that are traditionally associated with Alphonsus. One of Alphonsus's best known books is *The Glories of Mary*, so the first window honours the Blessed Virgin. The main image is mother and child with the dove representing the Holy Spirit at the top of the window. Beneath the larger image, there is a smaller one of Adam and Eve beside the tree in the Garden of Eden. The bands above and below the smaller image read (above) *O gloriosa virginum*, and (at the bottom), *sublimis inter sidera* ("O glorious virgin, splendid among the stars"). The scene in the garden is accompanied by an inscription in smaller letters: *Quod tristis Eva abstulit, tu redis almo germine* ("What we had lost in hapless Eve, your sacred womb again restores"). Both are quotations from the Latin hymn, *O gloriosa Domina*, once used in the divine office on Marian feasts.

The second window represents the Passion of Christ. Alphonsus was himself a skilled painter and several crucifixions he painted survive. The main representation is the crucifixion with Jesus accompanied by his mother and the beloved disciple. At the top of the picture is an image of the Lamb of God standing on the book with seven seals (Revelation 5:1, 6:1). The lower part represents Jesus in agony, comforted by the angel (Luke 22:39–43). The inscription on this window is *Copiosa apud eum redemptio* ("With him there is plentiful redemption", Psalm 130:7), the official motto of the Redemptorist Congregation.

The window above the altar represents the third great devotion of Alphonsus, to Jesus present in the Blessed Sacrament. Our view of this window is impeded by the altar. At the top, there is a representation of the traditional eucharistic symbol of "the pelican in her piety". Beneath it, Jesus stands, dressed in red and white and wearing a crown of thorns. Over the chalice, he holds the host, the symbols of eucharistic communion.

Coats of Arms of Archbishops of Westminster in the Windows

The North Aisle
We pass across the central aisle to the north aisle.

The north aisle was extended in 1929–30. It was impossible to match the south transept due to lack of ground, so the only workable solution was to extend St Gerard's chapel that had been erected in 1910 towards Clapham Park Road.

23. The Cardinals' Arms in the Windows
Most of the windows in the north aisle are in plain glass. Five of them contain a small inset panel containing the arms of the Archbishops of Westminster who at that time had been created cardinals. Only the initials of each are given on the window, so working from the end: FB (Francis Alphonsus Bourne), HV (Herbert Vaughan), HM (Henry Manning), NW (Nicholas Wiseman). Several of them had particularly warm relationships with the community of St Mary's. Wiseman had encouraged them to build in Clapham and had always remained a faithful friend: Herbert Vaughan's uncle was a Redemptorist (Fr Edmund Vaughan), and Bourne had been baptised and ordained in the church and made frequent retreats in the monastery.

24. The Shrine of Our Lady of Fatima
This is the most recent addition to the shrines and statues in the church. It is particularly dear to the Portuguese community who celebrate Mass in the church each week. The statues of the two children represent Francisco and Jacinta Marto, who together with their cousin Lucia, were the visionaries at Fatima in Portugal in 1917. They died at the age of eleven and ten respectively and were beatified in 2000.

25. The Ceiling

The ceiling of the new extension was markedly different from the rest of the church. It is flat and is made of carved oak. The only colour comes from the angels bearing the heraldic coats of arms. These are not easy to identify. First is that of the Redemptorist congregation, then Pope Pius XI, then in order the bishops of the diocese of Southwark from the restoration of the Catholic hierarchy to the time of the building of this extension. In reverse order, these are: Peter Amigo, Francis Bourne (later translated to Westminster), John Butt, Robert Aston Coffin (former Redemptorist provincial and rector of St Mary's), James Danell and Thomas Grant.

26. The Saint Gerard Window

Gerard Majella was a Redemptorist Brother who was born in the Kingdom of Naples in 1726 and died in 1755. Ill-health and poverty had prevented him from entering a religious community in his youth. He literally ran away from home and forced himself on a group of Redemptorist missioners who had come to his native Muro to preach a mission. Fearing that Gerard might make an attempt to join them, his mother had pleaded her dependence on his

St Gerard Majella Window detail: St Gerard cures a sick boy

small income as a tailor. On the advice of the leader of the mission band, she locked Gerard in his room, but he managed to escape, using his bed-clothes as a rope and leaving a note assuring his mother that he had run away to become a saint! He died at the age of twenty-nine, and despite advancing tuberculosis, the scourge of the time, he managed to become a most active member of the community, frequently travelling throughout the region to raise funds for the building of new monasteries. Even before his death, Gerard had acquired a reputation for working miracles. His life story – of a simple joyful young man with a generous heart – inspired many people who heard his story from the Redemptorists. He is particularly known as the patron saint of expectant mothers and fathers and his shrine is seldom without clients for his prayers.

The window was designed by Bentley to commemorate Gerard's beatification. It recounts eight incidents from his life. The upper row has four scenes. The first represents Gerard in ecstasy among the people: Gerard was a mystic, and incidents of ecstasy or total absorption in the things of God was a fairly common occurrence for him. The second scene is another ecstasy of Gerard's, this time in the presence of an image of the Passion. Gerard had a vivid sense of the reality of the Passion: as a teenager, he had persuaded the directors of the local passion play to allow him to play the part of Christ. So life-like was his performance that his mother fainted at the thought of what he might be suffering. In the third scene, Gerard saves a barrel of wine from going sour. For Italian country people, the loss of a year's wine could mean serious financial loss. Many of the stories of Gerard that entered the local folklore told how he had averted some serious damage or loss and highlighted the miraculous or unexpected. In the fourth scene, Gerard and Alphonsus meet. The darkest moment of Gerard's life came when he was charged with sexually abusing a young woman. Gerard remained silent. When the young woman was eventually forced to tell the truth, Gerard was asked by Alphonsus, his superior, to explain himself. It was probably the first time the two men met. Gerard said he had kept silent because the Rule, composed by Alphonsus, forbade the brethren to excuse themselves even when wrongly accused, imitating Christ who kept silent before Pilate. The silence the Rule asked for was in relatively minor things, not matters as serious as the charge made against Gerard.

The lower series of images relates to further scenes from the life of Gerard. Firstly, during a very severe local famine, Gerard fed countless poor people at the monastery door: even when it seemed the resources had more or less run out, Gerard always found something. The second shows how Gerard restored to health a boy who had fallen and seemed to have had a serious case of concussion. The third scene is Gerard rescuing the crew of a small boat in the Bay of Naples by walking boldly into the raging sea and dragging it to safety. The last scene depicts Gerard's final illness. A young boy is shown playing the harp. In the actual account, the boy could not play music but was fascinated by the harpsichord that had been brought into Gerard's room to lift his spirits as he could play a little. The legend that grew around the incident was that Gerard encouraged the boy to tinkle with the keys and he was soon able to produce a melody. The inscription on the top of the window reads *Potens apud Deum Gerardum advocatum cum fiducia* ("Gerard is a powerful advocate with God that you can trust").

27. The St Gerard Chapel

The St Gerard Chapel was designed by Osmond Bentley and was intended to balance his father's Lady Chapel on the opposite side of the church. Like it, it spans two arches and is enclosed by an iron grille. The heads from which the arches spring are St Alphonsus wearing a bishop's mitre (altar side) and St Clement in his Redemptorist habit. The middle arch rises from a shield bearing the initials "GM" (Gerard Majella). Our attention will be drawn first to the altar and the reredos. In the reredos, the wooden statue of Gerard depicts him clothed in his Redemptorist habit and holding a crucifix. Beneath the statue is a panel bearing the arms of the Redemptorist Congregation. Two pictures show scenes from the childhood of Gerard. That on the left recounts the story of Gerard and the lady. Close to Gerard's home village, there was a sanctuary of the Madonna where Gerard often went to play. When he returned in the evening, he usually had a little loaf of good quality white bread. To his mother's queries about where it came from, he replied he was given it by a lady whose little boy he had played with. That might have been a tale of everyday events, but later versions of the story suggest that the lady was in fact the Madonna and the little boy was the child Jesus. The second picture tells another story. In Gerard's time, children did not receive first communion until they were twelve or thirteen. Gerard once joined the people at the altar rails but the priest refused him. Next day, Gerard saw the priest and told him that St Michael the Archangel himself had brought him communion during the night! A child's dream or imagination at work? Perhaps, but there is no mistaking the devotion of the adult Gerard to the Eucharist.

The table of the altar is in red marble. The front is richly decorated with mother of pearl. The floor of the chapel also reflects its purpose. Some of the floor tiles have "GM"

Altar of St Gerard Majella

for Gerard Majella. On the step, a verse from the Beatitudes is intended to refer to Gerard: *Beati mundo corde: quoniam ipsi Deum videbunt* ("Blessed are the pure of heart, for they shall see God", Matthew 5:8).

On the side wall of the chapel there is a picture of another Redemptorist, St John Neumann (1811–1860). Born in Bohemia, John went as a young deacon on the American mission where he met the Redemptorists and joined the Congregation in 1840. He would have been a contemporary of the founders of Clapham: indeed, his novice master, the Austrian Joseph Prost, served some time in the Irish and English houses. Neumann was nominated as bishop of Philadelphia in 1852, at a time when emigrants were pouring into the United States. He was a simple man, but one with a strong pastoral sense and he began to build up in his diocese a structure to develop Catholic education. He was canonised in 1977.

28. The Apocalypse Window

A brightly coloured window is based on three scenes from the Book of Revelation. Working from the right hand side, in the first panel John the Seer of Revelation receives his commission from an angel to write in a book the things he is about to see (Revelation 1:10–11). In the second panel is depicted the complex vision of "one like a Son of Man". "Then I turned to see whose voice it was that spoke to me, and on turning I saw seven golden lamp-stands, and in the midst of the lamp-stands I saw one like the Son of Man, clothed with a long robe and with a golden sash across his chest. His head and his hair were white as white wool, white as snow; his eyes were like a flame of fire, his feet were like burnished bronze, refined as in a furnace, and his voice was like the sound of many waters. In his right hand he held seven stars, and from his mouth came a sharp, two-edged sword, and his face was like the sun shining with full force"(Revelation 1:12–16). Although the details of this account almost defy being visualised, our artist has made a serious attempt to transform the book's symbolic language into visual terms, so we can identify for example the seven stars in his hand, the sword coming from the mouth, the seven candlesticks. The third panel depicts the vision of the woman and the great red dragon (Revelation 12). Catholic tradition has usually identified the woman clothed with the sun (Revelation 12:1) as the Virgin Mary and the red dragon as Satan who will eventually be defeated by the Archangel Michael (Revelation 12:7).

We have no means of identifying the designer of this interesting, if somewhat unusual, window but it is dedicated to Elizabeth Sowberry.

29. The Statue of St Thérèse of Lisieux

Thérèse Martin was born in Alençon in France in 1873. She entered the Carmelite convent at Lisieux in 1888 at the age of fifteen. She died there in 1897. The publication of her journal, *The Story of a Soul*, after her death, made her very popular, She was canonised in 1925 and declared patron of the missions in 1927.

St Alphonsus Liguori, Founder of the Redemptorists

30. The Statue of St Alphonsus

Alphonsus Liguori was the founder of the Redemptorists. His chapel formerly stood where the organ is now. It was removed to the rear of the church and has already been visited in this guide (see south aisle).

31. The Window of the Saints

This window was part of an original chapel of St Alphonsus. Along with the great East Window, it was part of Wardell's design for the church. It is not easy to view it because of the organ. It depicts Saints Stanislaus Kostka and Aloysius (both regarded as patrons of young people), Patrick, Teresa of Avila, Francis Jerome (1642–1719, who had known Alphonsus as a child and they were canonised on the same day), John Nepomuk (1345–1393 of Bohemia, martyred because he refused to break the seal of the confessional), Philip Neri (1515–1595 founder of the Oratorian Congregation) and Francis Xavier (1506–1552, Jesuit missionary to the Far East and patron of the foreign missions).

Appendix
Work on the Church Spire 2015

Fergus McCormick B.Arch, RIBA, Dip.Prog.Management, AABC Senior Architect

Since 1998, concern had been expressed in successive five-yearly inspections about the deterioration of the stonework of the spire. This has led to the building being included on Historic England's list of "Heritage Buildings at Risk in the London area".

The spire is over 170 feet tall and is a major landmark in Clapham. It is largely constructed of Kentish ragstone, with a number of bands of York stone and the spire lights constructed of Bath stone. The tip of the spire was damaged during World War II by a barrage balloon, and was rebuilt in Portland stone in 1944.

In recent years, the condition of the stonework has continued to cause alarm. Close examination of the spire by steeplejacks confirmed the poor condition of much of the stonework. A protective fan was installed below the base of the spire to offer protection to church users and the public from falling stonework.

Due to the continuing deterioration in the spire stonework, the parish decided that major repair works were urgently required. The church applied in 2013 to the Heritage Lottery Fund for a repair grant under the "Places of Worship Grant Fund". The Heritage Lottery Fund confirmed the award of a first-round grant to the church in December 2013.

Thomas Ford and Partners were appointed as architects for the repair project following a competitive tender process. The design team was completed by the appointment of a structural engineer and quantity surveyor. Tender documents for the proposed repair works were issued to contractors experienced in conservation repair works in May 2014.

The first part of the contract consisted in the erection of a scaffold on the spire to facilitate detailed inspection of the stonework by the architect and structural engineer. PAYE Restoration Ltd was awarded the contract for erection of the scaffold which began in July 2014.

Appendix

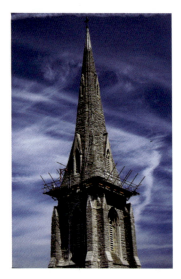

Following completion of the investigations works on site, the architect submitted the second-round submission to the Heritage Lottery Fund in December 2014, confirming the scope and costs of the repair works. The church received confirmation in March 2015 from the Heritage Lottery Fund of the second-stage grant approval for the spire repair works. The contract was signed with PAYE contractors and work on the spire repair began in May 2015

During the investigation stage, the architect found large areas on the spire where the ragstone walling had significantly deteriorated. A repair strategy was devised, which involved the removal of any loose sections of the face of the ragstone and of any sections of ragstone which were in exceptionally poor condition, with their replacement in new ragstone, matching the existing stonework.

Kentish ragstone is a distinctive, hard, sandy limestone. The stone has been used widely in the Greater London area and the South East of England throughout the centuries, particularly in medieval times. It was used on prominent historic buildings such as the Tower of London. The stone was also used extensively on church buildings during the Gothic Revival period in the nineteenth century when St Mary's church was constructed. In recent years it has been very difficult to source ragstone for repair of historic buildings but investment and expansion of the Hermitage Quarry in Maidstone has once again guaranteed supply of good quality ragstone for conservation repair works.

There are four York stone bands on the tower which are spaced at regular intervals on the spire. These bands perform a structural role in resisting the outward forces in the spire. The bands consist of sections of York stone which are connected by iron cramps. These cramps have rusted with time and have caused extensive damage to the York stone bands. The repair works involve the opening up and removal of the existing rusting cramps and their replacement with new stainless steel cramps. The badly damaged sections of existing York stone will be removed and replaced with new sections of York stone to match the existing ones.

The exterior stonework of the spire has been re-pointed several times since its construction. A sand and cement mortar mixture used for re-pointing in recent decades has exacerbated the deterioration of the ragstone. During the current repair work, areas of sound cement mortar will be retained, but damaged or loose sections will be removed and be re-pointed with fresh lime mortar. Lime mortar allows any moisture retained in the spire fabric to evaporate through the lime mortar join rather than through the adjoining stonework.

The existing spire lights are constructed of Bath stone. It was noted during the investigation stage, that a number of the capping stones that throw rainwater off the lights were badly eroded and needed replacement. As part of the repair works, the most badly eroded stones will be replaced with new Bath stone, matching the existing ones. Missing or badly eroded capping stones will also be replaced.

One of the conditions for receiving Heritage Lottery Fund grants is that knowledge gained on the local project be widely shared amongst conservation professionals and the local community. Thomas Ford and Partners have organised inspections of the spire by the following groups:

- AA Building Conservation Students
- Members of the Ecclesiastical Architects and Surveyors Association (EASA)
- Society for the Protection of Ancient Buildings (SPAB) Scholars and Fellows
- The Clapham Society
- The Churches Together in Clapham Group

The work now undertaken will guarantee the spire's structural integrity well into the future and will allow future generations to continue to worship in this wonderful ecclesiastical building and to enjoy its rich historic heritage.

12 October 2015

Acknowledgments

The photographs of St Mary's Church were taken by Jess Esposito, whom we thank most cordially for generously making them available for this guide.

I acknowledge my debt to the archivist of Clapham, Fr Jack Clancy C.Ss.R, who guided me through the holdings and pointed me towards many helpful books in the monastery library.

This project was originally commissioned by Fr Dominic O'Toole, then Parish Priest of St Mary's. To Fr Dominic, his successor Fr Richard Reid and the members of the Clapham community, especially Frs Michael McGreevy, Charles Corrigan, Beverly Ahearn, George Webster and Bro Thomas, I am indebted for their welcome and companionship, and especially for being the sources of the "living tradition" of St Mary's.

Apart from the church records of baptisms, marriages and the like, the *Provincial Chronicles* and the *Domestic Chronicles* of St Mary's were particularly helpful, being essentially an "observer participant" account of day to day life of the community and the church from the beginning.

The highly artistic design and arrangement of the contents of this book is the work of Anneke Calis of Tanika Design, Dublin.

The following printed sources were particularly helpful:

Kevin Callaghan: *The Glories of St Mary's Church, Clapham*. Redemptorists, Clapham, 2001.

A.G.Evans: *William Wardell: Building with Conviction*, Leominster, Herefordshire: Gracewing, 2011.

Winifride de l'Hôpital: *Westminster Cathedral and its Architect* (2 volumes), New York: Dodd, Mead and Co, 1919.

John Sharp: *Reapers of the Harvest: Redemptorists in Great Britain and Ireland, 1843-98*. Dublin: Veritas, 1991.

George Stebbing: *History of St Mary's, Clapham*. London: Sands and Co, 1935.

Website http://stmarys-clapham.org.uk
Email office@stmarys-clapham.org.uk